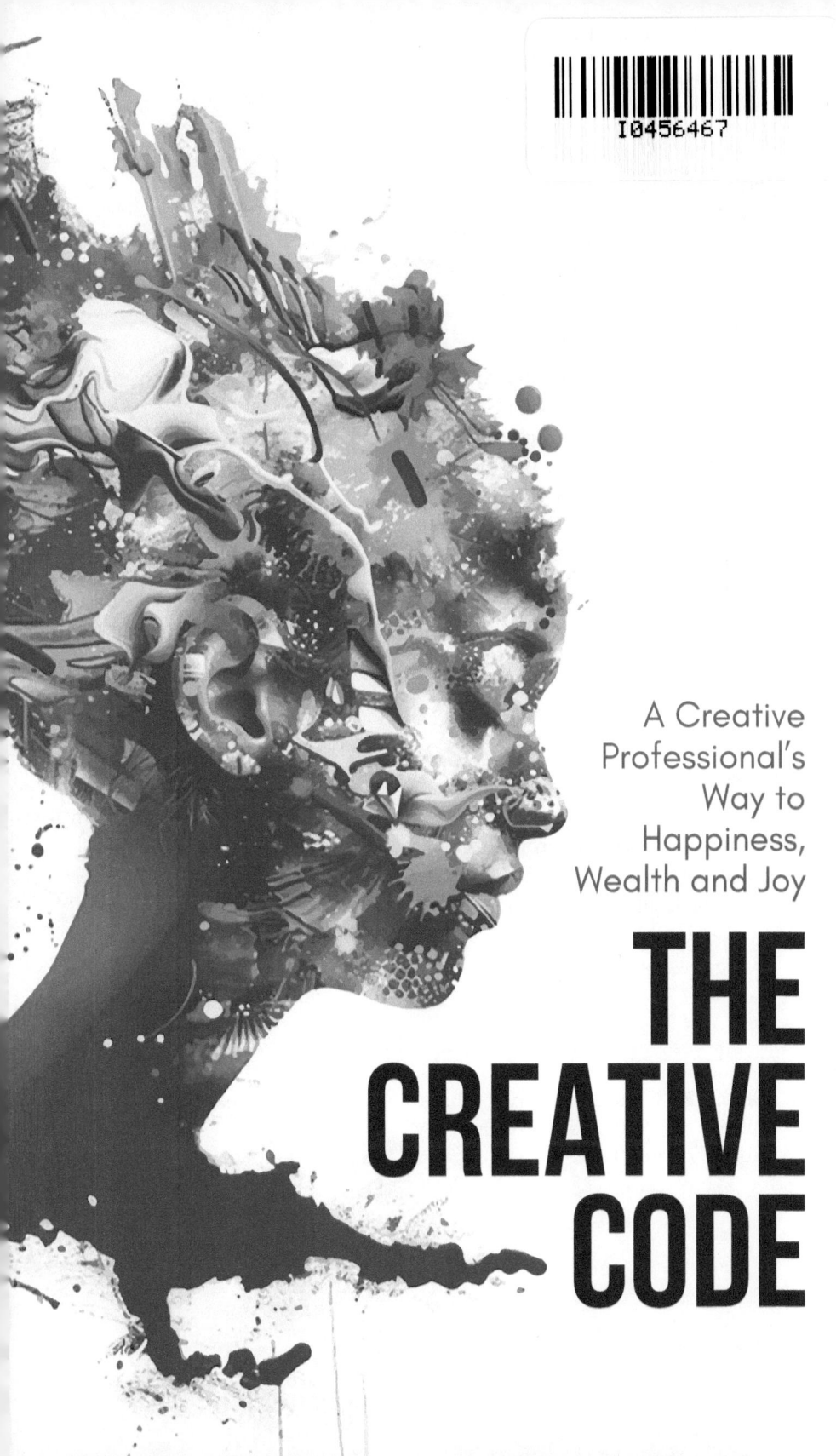

A Creative
Professional's
Way to
Happiness,
Wealth and Joy

THE
CREATIVE
CODE

Interior, Cover, Layout, and Graphic Design by Jen Fontanilla

Produced by Diamond Queen, LLC and Dr. Izdihar Jamil, Ph.D.

Disclaimer:

The author in no way, shape, or form considers any of the information in
this book to be advice, promise, guarantee, warranty, or any form of professional advice. It is intended for informational and educational purposes
only. The results produced by the author, or anyone referenced in the book,
are mentioned for illustration purposes only and are not intended to imply
or suggest that you will have results that are at all similar to those in the
book.

ISBN: 979-8-9907213-1-9 (Paperback)
ISBN: 979-8-9907213-2-6 (Hardcover)
ISBN: 979-8-9907213-0-2 (Epub)

TO CHRISTOPHER JORDAN

Dream big and take magnificent action to make your reality
full of love, joy, wealth, abundance, and prosperity
— however you choose to define it.

You inspire me to become a better human being every single day.

I love you.

TO KISMA

For your wisdom, guidance, experience, and teachings. The impact and
difference you have made in my life is immeasurable. I am grateful for you
— for your belief in me and for reminding me of what is always possible.

TO ALL THE DREAMERS, THE VISIONARIES, AND THE CREATORS

This book is for you — the visual artists, performing artists, writers,
craftspeople, filmmakers and videographers, designers, musicians and
composers, culinary artists, architects and urban planners, multimedia artists
and makers who breathe life into the world through
your unique expressions and ideas.

Your creativity is a gift that shapes the fabric of our lives,
adds color to our days, and sparks inspiration in hearts and minds everywhere.

May you always find the courage to share your gifts, the confidence to know
your worth, and the strength to pursue your passions with unwavering faith.
Remember that your work has the power to transform, heal, and uplift.

Here's to your endless imagination, your boundless spirit,
and the beauty you bring to the world.

I am tremendously grateful for you.

• • •

THE CREATIVE CODE

Finally, a book on money and prosperity that makes sense to a creative mind. Jen has a gift for integrating the left and the right brain showing that inspiration and practicality can co-exist, especially when it comes to our finances. Her stories beautifully capture the struggles we experience as creatives and serve as proof that we're not doomed to the starving artists cliché. Not only will readers get to the root of their financial woes, Jen also gives tangible action steps to conquer those pesky financial blocks that unconsciously block creativity...for good. Buckle up! Your beliefs about money are going to be flipped, twisted and turned inside out.

Elisa Estrera
Brand Strategist and Emotional Alchemist of Vivid Edge - yourvividedge.com
@yourvividedge, linkedin.com/elisa_estrera

An inspiring blend of financial savvy and artistic pursuit, this book offers a refreshing perspective on turning creative passions into a sustainable career. It's a must-read for anyone seeking to balance the practicalities of money with the boundless possibilities of their creative talents!

Lance Orion
Music Producer

"The Creative Code" is a transformative journey through the intricacies of the artist's world, a must-read for anyone dedicated to their craft. As an artist myself, I found its insights deeply relatable, particularly in its exploration of the origins of our sense of value. The book eloquently addresses the damaging notion that there's no financial viability in art, a belief that can erode our self-worth and confidence.

What sets "The Creative Code" apart is its practicality. It doesn't just dwell on the challenges; it offers tangible strategies for navigating them. From delving into universal laws to reshaping our relationship with money, the book provides a roadmap for transforming our reality and laying the groundwork for financial prosperity.

One aspect I truly appreciate is its emphasis on building a support system and team. By fostering a community that believes in our artistic vision, we can cultivate abundance together.

Overall, "The Creative Code" is a groundbreaking achievement that will resonate deeply within the creative community. It has the power to reignite our passion and spark a paradigm shift in how artists are valued and compensated. It's not just a book; it's a catalyst for change that will shape the future of creativity for generations to come.

Lyn Pacificar
Shamanic Artist/CEO Founder of Herbalaria
@lynpacificar_art @iamherbalaria @katuuran_lyn

• • •

"The Creative Code" is THE book I wish I had when I took the plunge to leave my successful career in construction to pursue a career in art. Even though I have always been good with financial planning and management, I didn't realize how many money mindset blocks I had that stopped me from valuing my work as an artist and creative. If I had Jen's book back then, my journey to identify and dismantle these limitations, finally allowing me to value my work as an artist, would have been way smoother. Only when I started shifting my limiting money beliefs and aligning my actions with principles & Universal Laws Jen talks about in her book, I started seeing the positive shift in the financial success of my creative business. It's easy to shift a mindset, but difficult to sustain it when it's dealt with on a superficial level. And that's what Jen's book will help you do. Unlike many finance books overloaded with generic advice, this book dives deep. It's written by a creative, for creatives! Jen gets the specific roadblocks artists face and offers practical tools tailored to our unique needs. Forget fleeting mindset shifts or budgeting tricks; it will equip you with lasting strategies to overcome money blocks and build a thriving creative practice. From practical steps of how to create a better financial plan, to resolving the deep-seated money blocks, this book is your ultimate guide to ditching the starving artist syndrome and embracing the love of abundance and freedom you desire and deserve.

Loveleen Saxena
Artist + Founder - LOVELEEN®
@loveleen.saxena

J en's story is highly relatable as I am also a first born, first generation Filipino-American who experienced the inherent pressures of maintaining financial security while upholding cultural expectations and traditions. I always knew deep down I wanted something else out of life, and going all in on my artistic passions was how I ultimately realized making a living against the grain was entirely possible. "The Creative Code" is a real life testimonial and guide to achieving success—and thriving in your artistic endeavors. Highly recommend for anyone that is on the fence about taking that leap. It could be the nudge you need to change your life!

Jeremy Buenaobra
Tailor/Designer of Goodwork
@goodwork_tailoring

J en is a genius as she gives you the code to unlock your life's creative expression. Actionable steps right away? Say less! This is a paradigm shifter. You will thank Jen later.

Oma Singh
Copywriter

An essential read for artists and creatives functioning outside the "norms" of a 9-5 world. An essential tool to help navigate the often unpredictable peaks and valleys experienced by creative freelancers, specifically, with regard to money. "The Creative Code" is a reference to be highlighted, underlined and occasionally referenced, when doubt, frustration and lack of hope take hold of an idle mind to help calm the soul. Can I make a living as an artist? Can I make more money doing what I do as a creative? How do I save, invest and maximize my earnings as an artist? How to maintain a positive money mind state and faith when it comes to the (yet to arrive) next big job around the corner? All of these questions are more easily "deciphered" within.

Paul Sanders
Actor/Voice Talent/Writer
www.PaulSandersVO.com

This book is a game-changer for artists ready to boss up and start their own gig. It's like your personal mentor- packed with the inspo and know-how you need to crush it in the creative and entrepreneurial world. Must- read!

Jun Pinon "The Flower Picasso"
Floral Designer
@jun_pinon @flower_picasso

DON'T FORGET TO TAKE WHAT YOU LEARN IN "THE CREATIVE CODE" TO THE NEXT LEVEL...

Grab your bonus materials below!

- ✅ Creative Soul Ascension Meditation
- ✅ Higher Self Meditation to tap into your deepest creative powers
- ✅ "Rewriting Your Money Story" Workbook
- ✅ the ultimate checklist to build your financial team
- ✅ and more!

JUST SCAN THE QR CODE RIGHT HERE OR VISIT THE LINK BELOW TO ACCESS YOUR FREE BONUSES!

SCAN ME

www.jenmoneycoach.com/the-creative-code-book-bonuses

For more information about transforming your money mindset or to learn more about how you can achieve financial prosperity as a creative, make sure to visit **www.jenmoneycoach.com**

THE CREATIVE CODE
TABLE OF CONTENTS

PART I: FOUNDATIONS OF YOUR MONEY MINDSET

Introduction

Understanding Universal Laws and How They Influence Our Money

Understanding Your Current Relationship With Money

PART II: TRANSFORMING YOUR MONEY MINDSET

Rewriting Your Money Story

The Power of Forgiveness and Letting Go

Making Space for Creativity and Abundance

• • •

PART III: BUILDING A POSITIVE RELATIONSHIP WITH MONEY

Cultivating Self-Worth and Valuing Yourself

Overcoming Fear and Embracing Your Value

PART IV: DAILY PRACTICES FOR A PROSPEROUS LIFE

Implementing Daily Practices for Growth

PART V: PLANNING FOR NOW AND TOMORROW

Creating a Prosperity Plan

The Art of Abundance - Rediscovering Your Creative Essence

"The journey from crayon-filled pages to the canvas of our lives reminds us that the art of creation is not just an act of passion, but a testament to our boundless potential for abundance."

JEN FONTANILLA

"It's Coloring Day!" As a child, the mere mention of it by my third-grade teacher would set my heart racing with excitement. Coloring Day wasn't just an activity; it was the day my soul felt most alive. Armed with crayons and paints, I embarked on adventures, mixing colors to discover new shades as if by magic. It was my first taste of creation, of bringing something into existence that had lived only in my imagination. The joy and freedom I felt during those moments were unmatched. Coloring Day represented a world of possibilities, a reminder that joy could be found in the simple act of creation.

The Shift Away from My Essence

As the years passed, the world told me that Coloring Day was just a childish distraction. I found myself pursuing a path far removed from the vibrant creativity of my youth. I ended up working in a hospital, a place where the color seemed to drain from the world, replaced by the stark reality of life and death. The satisfaction and joy of releasing my creativity were gone, replaced by a logical, rational approach to life that left me feeling confused and, most profoundly, empty. The vibrant colors of my childhood dreams faded into the background of a life chosen by practicality over passion.

Then, a chance encounter with a friend and a colorful flier he had created in Photoshop reignited the spark I thought I'd lost. It was as if someone had opened the windows to my soul, letting light flood into forgotten corners. The excitement, the aliveness I felt in that moment, was a beacon calling me back to my true self! It was Coloring Day all over again, but this time, it paved the way for my future.

My Mission

This pivotal moment was more than a personal revelation; it became the cornerstone of my mission to support creatives. As a graphic designer for almost 25 years and 19 years in financial services, formerly as a financial advisor and now a Certified Money Coach (CMC)®, speaker, and author, I've witnessed firsthand the struggles creatives face in valuing their work and claiming their worth. My heart aches for those who've been led to believe their passion can't sustain them.

I've heard the words that crush creatives' dreams and hearts. What hurts the most is hearing from our own parents, family, or friends, "When are you going to get a real job?" Delegating any type of creative field to a hobby instead of a legitimate means to make a living. Why can't we live out our passions that fuel us and give us life? So, what if I don't want to choose a traditional route? Yet, often, the important people in our lives define what a "regular, real, normal job" is. I have seen from friends, clients, and others who have shared their stories with me that this seems to be even more prevalent in immigrant families. Culture, societal pressure, lack of understanding, and hard-wired money stories all play a part in the whole narrative against creativity as a valid career.

We don't have to buy into the narrative of the Starving Artist anymore because there is another way.

Why Money Mindset Matters for Creatives

Understanding and transforming our money mindset is crucial, especially for creatives. It's not just about learning to manage finances but about recognizing the value of our work and the worth of our contributions. It's about believing that we can do this because it feels right, and it's what we want to do regardless of the various voices telling us how to live our lives.

My journey has shown me that the stories we tell ourselves about money can either confine us or free us. I believe deeply in the potential of every creative soul to not only live out their artistic passions but to thrive financially while doing so.

My commitment to empowering creatives stems from a profound understanding of the challenges we face in a world that often undervalues art or any type of creative work. I've felt the sting of skepticism and the raised eyebrows when choosing a path less traveled. Yet, my experiences from Coloring Day to the present have taught me that creativity is not just a part of life; it is life itself. Creatives hold the power to envision and shape the world in ways others can't imagine. I believe in the worthiness of creatives to achieve financial abundance. It's about helping people love what they do, showing them how to trust and listen to their inner guidance in their decisions, leaning into their greater potential, and gaining the confidence that comes from knowing you can do whatever you want to do by living out your full potential, your life's creative work and make money (and lots of it!) **You CAN have it all, and I truly believe that.**

This book is more than a guide; it's a call to action for every artist, designer, musician, dancer, and dreamer who has ever doubted their worth. If you've ever questioned whether you could really do this or if you should, this is for you—the creative. It's a manifesto for changing the narrative around creativity and money, for stepping into our power as creators of beauty and value. Together, we can rewrite our money stories, not just for ourselves but for generations of creatives to come. We are worthy of Coloring Day, every day, and the abundance it can bring into our lives.

Are you prepared to think creatively and redefine what success means to you?

Embrace Your Journey to Abundance

You're about to embark on a transformative path that will redefine your relationship with money and reconnect you with the abundant universe. It's a journey where creativity and prosperity coexist, where your artistic essence is celebrated and seen as the key to unlocking boundless abundance. This isn't about chasing dollars; it's about harmonizing with the universe's boundless generosity, making financial well-being a natural extension of your artistic journey.

A Tale of Awakening

Remember your own version of Coloring Day and the joy you felt during art days back when you were growing up and got to draw, cut, glue, and just create? It was that unadulterated happiness found in the magic of mixing colors and creating something from nothing. It's the essence of our creative spirit. Yet, somewhere along the line, we've been conditioned to believe this spirit won't sustain us, that our dreams are too lofty for the real world. Or even worse, we were told that those were cute hobbies or fun things to do but not serious enough to make a living from them. But the moment I rediscovered my passion for design, I awakened to a profound truth: within each of us lies infinite potential, not just for creativity but for abundance.

The Universe's Bounty

This book is an invitation to explore your inherent connection to abundance and discover that creating wealth is as natural as breathing for those who align with God's or the universe's (whatever your word is) generosity. Money isn't reserved for a chosen few. It's accessible to all who harness their inner talents and venture beyond traditional limitations. There is a path toward a life where abundance flows freely, and money is a joyous outcome of living in harmony with universal principles.

You are a magnificent being. You are a spiritual being having a physical experience, capable of tapping into the universe's unlimited abundance. This journey will reveal that creating money and prosperity can be as effortless as expressing your true self. By embracing the spiritual laws of money, unlimited thinking, giving, receiving, and more—you'll discover that abundance is about fulfillment, not just accumulation. Money will become a joyful companion on your path to expressing your soul's desires.

• • •

Aligning with Your Higher Self

In these pages, you'll be guided to connect with your Higher Self to become a beacon of magnetism for your highest good. Your Higher Self is also regarded as your superior self, your soul, the aspect of you that is linked to the God-force, the God-within, or the profound segment of your existence. The true essence of your being, the core of who you are, is the ultimate source of prosperity. It's not your analytical, reasoning mind that holds power; rather, it's the God-spark presence within you. When your focus shifts to this foundational Source, to the cause itself, abundance naturally follows. The deeper and more personal your connection with the true Source of your wealth, and the closer you become to your divine self, the more abundance will flow into your life.

Each concept here transcends mere mental understanding. You will need to apply these concepts and take a leap of faith into trusting in God's abundance. As your trust transforms into conviction, you'll effortlessly attract not just wealth but the very essence of what you desire for a fulfilled life.

Mastering the Flow of Abundance

Through mastery of these principles, you'll learn to welcome and release money, objects, and situations with grace, allowing each to serve your higher purpose at the perfect time. This is about letting go and letting flow—welcoming new opportunities with open arms and saying goodbye to what no longer serves you. It's about making choices that reflect your highest values and letting your life be a testament to your unique creative spirit. As you align more closely with your soul, your creativity and ideas will flourish, leading to greater abundance in every aspect of your life.

A Symphony of Spiritual and Material Harmony

When followed, the spiritual laws of money and abundance enhance one's life work and contribute to the collective good. By embracing cooperation over competition, honoring the Earth, and letting one's actions be guided by one's higher self, money and abundance will flow into one's life with ease. This journey is about recognizing the sacred interplay between one's spiritual path and material existence, allowing each to enrich the other.

Invitation to a Life of Abundance

Consider this your invitation to a grand adventure, one where every chapter nudges you closer to a life where creativity and prosperity dance together in harmony. Set your intention now to welcome abundance, to be open to the universe's gifts, and to step into your power as a creator of your own reality.

Your Creative Renaissance

So, dear creator, as you stand on the threshold of this new chapter, remember that your capacity for creation is boundless. The universe is inviting you to co-create a reality of unmatched abundance, where your creative passions are not just viable but vital to the world's tapestry. Let this be the moment you reclaim your Coloring Day, the moment you step into the full spectrum of your potential.

Embrace this journey with an open heart and an expansive mind. The path ahead is vibrant, abundant, and utterly transformative. Welcome to your renaissance, where every stroke of your brush paints a new world of possibility.

I will even suggest that this would be a great time to consider getting a journal purely dedicated to this journey so you can take notes, journal about some of the questions here, and reflect on your thoughts as you go along this ride.

A Few Important Notes

I need to tell you what this book isn't about. This isn't another money book about financial planning or how to create a budget. (Trust me, there are plenty of great books out there about all that stuff.)

This is totally different and deeper than that. Yes, I believe in the importance of financial literacy. (Remember, I used to be a financial advisor, so I have a genuine appreciation for that work.) But what got me curious over the years was wondering why some people could stick to a plan, why others would blow it, and why change only happened for some and not others.

It would be several years later that I discovered these principles and ways of thinking, which I am sharing with you now. These principles held many of the answers to those questions I had years ago. Traditional financial planning and advising don't dive into these principles or your subconscious patterns. The problem is not that you're bad with money. You just didn't know or were not ever taught how to get to the root of the problem.

When you look behind the numbers, take a deeper look into who you are, understand why you make the financial decisions that you do, and have the thoughts that you do, you can begin to unlock the puzzle.

As you go along this journey, I want you to ask yourself, what does wealth mean to you anyway? As a society, we have predominantly been trained to define wealth as having a lot of money or a certain kind of profession, job, business, or career. To me, wealth is about having prosperity in ALL areas of your life. And I want to help you change that narrative if that is the definition that you have been striving for. You can have it all.

One more thing.

This journey we're about to embark on together… it's not tied to any one religion or faith. Instead, think of it as an exploration of teachings and universal laws that exist to enrich our lives, regardless of our background or beliefs. So, as we dive into these pages together, I encourage you to stay curious, ask questions, and keep an open mind. Don't worry about agreeing with everything I say—heck, the beauty of this journey lies in our diversity of thought and experience. What I do ask is that you approach this adventure without judgment, open to the possibilities that lie beyond your current horizon.

Who knows? You might just discover something incredibly enriching about the universe, creativity, and, yes, even about yourself. Let's explore with open hearts and minds, ready to be surprised by what we find.

Now, let's go make a masterpiece. Are you ready?

Action Step:

Take a moment to write a powerful commitment to yourself in your journal or somewhere you will see it daily.

You can use one of the following commitments or craft your own unique promise:

> *"I commit to embracing my artistic passion with open arms, forging a path where creativity and wealth flourish together."*

> *"Today, I set a vow to myself: To let my creativity lead the way to abundance, ensuring that my artistic pursuits are not just passions but the source of my wealth."*

> *"I dedicate myself to nurturing my creative talents, believing firmly that through them, I will unlock the door to endless prosperity."*

This written commitment will serve as your guiding light on the journey ahead, reminding you of your promise to blend your creativity with prosperity.

2   Living Life by the Universal Laws

*"Let your actions be your message to God and the universe,
a declaration of your intent and a magnet for miracles."*

JEN FONTANILLA

Reflecting on my early days as a financial advisor back in 2006, I was once subtly asked, as if uncovering a profound secret, "Have you ever watched 'The Secret?'" I responded, "No, I haven't. Is it something I should explore?" The fear of missing out on something groundbreaking started there.

This was essentially my first encounter with the concept of universal laws, highlighted through The Law of Attraction as showcased in the movie. This experience ignited a curiosity within me to explore beyond the surface of this singular law. I came to realize that the realm of universal laws was vast, encompassing several core principles. I aim to share insights into twelve of these foundational laws and their significance.

What I find fascinating is that, prior to my formal exploration of these laws, I was unconsciously applying some of them in my life without explicit knowledge. Looking back, I can now connect the dots and understand the reasons behind why certain encounters ended with success and how they seemed to manifest with relative ease.

I would enter any interview for a new graphic design position with confidence. It was a game for me. Honestly, when I interviewed at some places, I had absolutely no experience! I secretly told myself, "I'll figure it out. Heck, what do I have to lose?" I wasn't attached to the outcome. I would often say, "If I get it, great! If I don't, no problem. Let's just see what's possible." I didn't worry about what I didn't know. I made sure I smiled and focused on what I did know and what I was good at: an eagerness to learn and that I was that team player we all say we are on our resumes! With a conscious grasp of these laws and how to engage with them, it becomes evident that we can navigate our world with a newfound sense of empowerment and possibility.

These principles extend far beyond mere strategies for financial gain; they integrate deeply into our very essence, fostering a sense of balance, purpose, and a profound connection with the universe itself. As we explore each Universal Law, consider them as guides accompanying you on your creative journey, showing you how to attract prosperity, draw in clients who truly align with your vision, and shape a career or business that not only sustains you financially but also brings deep fulfillment.

Understanding and applying these Universal Laws can transform not only how we approach our financial goals and client relationships but also enhance our personal and professional development. They empower creative individuals to nurture a career that resonates with the universal currents of energy and abundance, creating a life that is not just about making a living but about living with meaning.

1. **The Law of Divine Oneness:** *Everything in the Universe is Interconnected*

This law is a nudge that every thought and action of ours sends vibes across the cosmic web, reminding us that we're all part of something way bigger. When you're getting creative, whether it's with your art, music, or any project, remember you're tapping into a massive collective energy. What you create doesn't just end with you; it ripples out, impacting others in ways you might not see coming. Your work can inspire, heal, or spark joy, and that's the beauty of Divine Oneness in your creative journey.

For anyone in the creative field, this law encourages us to think about the energy we're sending out. It's like viewing your work as a piece of the huge human tapestry. This mindset can not only elevate the vibe of what we put out there but also draw in clients who dig what you're about, boosting your work through vibes that match up.

Quick tip: Let your creative intentions vibe with the positive changes you want to see. Aiming to inspire courage? Channel that bravery into your work. And it's all about aiming for a collective impact rather than just personal success.

Take Alex as an example: by linking local artists with businesses needing creative juice, he showed how embracing our connectedness not only helps others grow but also boosts our own path.

So, remember, your creativity isn't just about you. It's a contribution to the bigger picture. By leaning into the Law of Divine Oneness, you're not just making art; you're actively shaping the future. Think of yourself as not just an artist but a part of a grand network of creation. Your work is important, echoing far beyond your own space.

2. The Law of Vibration: *Every Entity in the Universe Vibrates at a Specific Frequency*

Everything in our universe is vibrating at its core. This concept is quite profound. Even what appears solid is, at a microscopic level, in constant motion with atoms vibrating. This vibration gives off a frequency, or what we might also refer to as energy. It's fascinating to consider ourselves, including our clients and everything in our lives, as entities of energy. Pierre Teilhard de Chardin, a renowned French philosopher, once observed, "We are spiritual beings having a physical experience," capturing the essence of our vibrational existence.

Consider Michelle's story: a freelance writer who decided to shift her mindset from one of scarcity to abundance, focusing on gratitude and the unique value she offers. By consciously elevating her vibrational energy through optimism and professionalism, she witnessed a noticeable growth in her clientele, many of whom remarked on the positive energy they perceived in her work. Michelle's experience underscores the idea that aligning our vibrational frequency with our aspirations can naturally expand our business to mirror this enhanced energy.

As creative professionals, we have the power to elevate our vibration through positive thoughts and actions, thus attracting clients, opportunities, and income that resonate with our heightened frequency. The way we present ourselves in our business is ultimately how our business presents itself to the world. Adopting a limited perspective yields limited results, whereas embracing our potential and showing up confidently can lead to significant growth. If we're ever dissatisfied with our current business outcomes, adjusting our vibration is a powerful place to start.

3. The Law of Correspondence: *The Outer World Reflects Your Inner World*

Your life's external circumstances naturally align with your internal state and beliefs, much like how a movie projected on a screen reflects its film reel. The clarity of our perceptions—our "lens"—also plays a crucial role in how we interpret and engage with the world around us. For creatives, harboring an abundance and success mindset can directly influence their reality, attracting more rewarding opportunities and financial growth.

Now, consider the journey of a digital marketing team navigating a period of relentless deadlines and challenging clients, a scenario that seemed to perpetuate a cycle of stress and scarcity. Recognizing the external turmoil as a reflection of their internal state, they pivoted towards cultivating a collective atmosphere of abundance and positivity.

This shift in mindset proved transformative. As their internal vibrations rose, the nature of the opportunities that came transformed dramatically. They began attracting projects that were not only more lucrative but also more enjoyable. This evolution was a testament to the principle that our external world is a mirror of our internal landscape, illustrating how a change in collective mindset can significantly alter a team's professional trajectory.

• • •

4. **The Law of Attraction:** *What You Expect to Manifest is What You Will Manifest*

This principle reveals the magnetic power of our expectations, guiding us like a GPS toward our desired destinations. For creative professionals, it unlocks a realm of endless possibilities, making positive outcomes more than just daydreams; they become attainable realities.

Jamie, a graphic designer, began visualizing each project as a pathway to greater success, embodying the Law of Attraction by focusing on what and why without sweating the how or when. The shift Jamie made not only brought them profitable projects but also highlighted the importance of aligning mindsets with aspirations.

As you chart your path in the creative world, cultivate an abundance and success mindset. Visualize your desired outcomes and trust the journey. By expecting success and focusing on what you want, you become a magnet for opportunities that align with your greatest ambitions, co-creating a fulfilling journey with the universe.

5. **The Law of Inspired Action:** *Manifestation Requires Action*

It's one thing to dream big and set intentions; it's another to move your feet. This law serves as a gentle nudge, reminding us that our dreams and goals aren't just going to fall into our laps—we've got to reach out and pull them closer. For those of us in the creative realm, this means that our aspirations for financial prosperity and professional growth need to be met with concrete steps.

Whether it's putting yourself out there with marketing, networking to find new clients, or honing your craft with further education and practice, every step is a deliberate move toward the future you're aiming to create. Those with a creative mindset have a special advantage in this context in how we approach these actions, making them not just necessary steps but an extension of our creative expression.

For Sam, a freelance illustrator, this meant overhauling their portfolio, engaging with potential clients on social media, and enhancing their skills through a digital course. Taking proactive measures not only brought Sam's dreams closer to reality but also highlighted the effectiveness of taking action that aligns with your aspirations.

Remember, the Law of Inspired Action isn't about busywork. It's about meaningful, purpose-driven efforts that bridge the gap between where you are now and where you want to be. It's about embracing the journey, knowing that each step, no matter how small, is a crucial part of the manifestation process. One thing that is super important to mention is that when it comes to manifesting, we can't assume that all we have to do is just think our way to abundance. It doesn't work that way. We are required to co-create with God, Source, or the universe, do our part, and take action.

6. The Law of Perpetual Transmutation of Energy: *Higher Vibrations Consume and Transform Lower Ones*

This relates to moving energy around to create something new—we can create anything out of nothing.

We can turn poverty into wealth, and our businesses can help other people make a living. So here you are, sitting in these chairs, thinking about either jumping into starting your own business or building your career and just deciding to really go for it. Think about how many people's lives you're touching with your business or could touch.

You have your team's back, and you are going to make a significant impact on your customers' lives. You're going to change your students' lives. It's incredible what can happen when you make a deliberate decision to shuffle around energy in order to make something new. Energy shifts based on where you put your intention and focus, and it's all tied to the Law of Attraction, Law of Vibration, and all those other big laws.

You can overcome any negative experience by transmuting it into something positive. Have you ever dealt with unsupportive family members or a spouse or partner, co-worker, and judgment? Sometimes, people are waiting to support you or believe in you when you're successful. But you can't wait for that. You can't wait for the approval. We must always show up for ourselves first and prove to ourselves that it is possible.

Casey transformed their struggling design studio by embracing the Law of Perpetual Transmutation of Energy, shifting from negativity to brainstorming positive and innovative strategies. This pivot not only revived their business but also created a ripple effect, helping other small businesses thrive and embodying the power of positive energy transformation.

If we wait for others to believe in our dreams before we do, you will be the one living with the consequences of not living out your dreams. Not them. Your energy and how you approach all of this will allow you to overcome the lack of support.

Be the CEO of your own energy.

This is a game of managing and directing your own energy.

7. The Law of Cause and Effect (The Law of Karma): *Every Action has a Reaction*

Everything always, always comes back to you. I firmly, firmly believe that by being the best version of you and doing the right thing always, and that just means doing the best that you can with the resources that you have. If you do that, you can trust that you'll always be taken care of.

Treat other businesses the way you'd love to be treated by your customers, clients, or vendors.

Anytime we're dealing with a challenge or anytime we're dealing with a low moment, or anytime we're struggling with a difficult client or a difficult customer or a difficult team member going through a challenge, I just rely on the fact that if you keep doing the right thing and continue to be the best version of yourself, the universe will always come through. When we can lean on God to take care of us, we don't need to worry.

Riley, a dedicated freelance photographer, adhered to the principle "do good, and good will come to you," despite facing challenges with difficult clients and project obstacles, always prioritizing high-quality work and respect. Their commitment to professionalism and ethics boosted their reputation, leading to an increase in referrals and a significant improvement in both income and job satisfaction. Riley's experience exemplifies the Law of Cause and Effect: positive actions and professionalism yield success and stability.

For creatives, investing time and resources into their skills and business will lead to greater income and success. Efficiently managing finances and reinvesting in their craft can produce beneficial financial effects.

8. The Law of Compensation: *You Receive What You Give*

This is like the Law of Cause and Effect but from a monetary perspective. The biggest mistake that people make here is that they don't realize that they must give value for money.

Opening a business doesn't mean you'll wake up the next day with a million dollars in your bank account. To really make it work, you need to enrich people's lives. This often means creating loads of free content to draw people in. They won't just magically appear at your doorstep. The key is to always be the one to give first.

> *"You will get all that you want in life.*
> *If you help enough people get what they want."*
>
> ZIG ZIGLAR

In the competitive content creation arena, a small team is committed to delivering exceptional value through their work, focusing on enriching their audience's experience without immediate expectations of return. Their investment in creating high-quality, free content transformed their blog and social media into sought-after resources, significantly expanding their audience and revenue. This strategy of generosity catalyzed their success, attracting lucrative partnerships and building a devoted fanbase, exemplifying the Law of Compensation: the more you give, the more you receive.

Creatives who provide immense value through their work and interactions are more likely to be compensated generously, attracting clients willing to pay for their high-quality services.

9. The Law of Relativity: *Each Person's Journey is Different*

Everyone will face challenges as opportunities for growth. We can live with confidence, adopt a curious mindset, and view these challenges as a reality check that brings out our higher self.

We need to have perspective because nothing is ever as bad as it seems. Life is constantly happening for us. And challenges do not mean you're doing something wrong. They're actually teaching you lessons that are invaluable and crucial to your success. Challenges are here to serve us. Our work or businesses are here to help others and usually with their problems. We are all problem solvers. How can we expect to have a business or the work that we do without problems? It's good to have problems because they are our teachers. They could sometimes be our biggest blessings.

During a challenging year filled with setbacks, Jordan, a web designer, applied the Law of Relativity, interpreting these obstacles as personalized growth opportunities rather than reasons for despair. By adopting a mindset of curiosity and analysis, Jordan transformed their trials into lessons on business, creativity, and resilience, enhancing their portfolio and skills. This approach not only fostered personal development but also attracted projects that matched their newly refined abilities and outlook, proving that viewing challenges as pathways to growth can reveal one's higher self and lead to distinct success.

Creative professionals should focus on their progress and not compare their financial success to others. This mindset helps maintain motivation and attract opportunities suited to their unique path.

10. The Law of Polarity: *Everything Has an Opposite*

You will always get what you don't want so that you can gain clarity on what you want. Remember the problems we wish we didn't have? Sometimes, the answers to what you want come from the journey; learning the hard lessons through the process may be just what you need to achieve what you desire. The answers we seek often arrive in unexpected ways. We may anticipate clear directions or an easy path, but the reality is usually different. Frequently, gaining wisdom and insight necessitates enduring painful or challenging experiences. These lessons lead us to reflect and ultimately discover the answers we desire.

We often believe we end up with the opposite of what we're after because we messed up, or life's just terrible, or things just keep happening to us, or, you know, insert any grievance here. But in reality, all this strengthens us.

Stop giving things more power than they truly hold over your life. There is power in asking and asking. What do I not want? Opposites serve us by bringing us a new level of appreciation for our desires. Opposites serve us by bringing us a new level of appreciation for our desires.

Facing many setbacks in their debut major project, Alex, an independent filmmaker, encountered underfunding, missed deadlines, and team discord, attracting the opposite of their desires. However, by applying the Law of Polarity, Alex viewed these hurdles not as failures but as essential contrasts that clarified their needs for successful projects, such as improved planning, effective communication, and team alignment. This perspective shift led to their next project's success, securing proper funding and a harmonious team, affirming that every challenge contains the potential for growth and achieving one's creative goals.

Knowing that the potential for abundance exists, creatives facing financial difficulties can find solace by focusing on positive financial strategies and mindsets to achieve it.

11. The Law of Rhythm: *Nature is Seasonal and Cyclical*

You can't keep pushing at full throttle all the time. Even if you think you're invincible, burnout is lurking around the corner. Life, like nature, has its seasons for a reason. Your business will go through cycles, too. Sometimes, you'll feel like you're just staring at the ground, waiting for something—anything—to happen. It feels like watching paint dry, and you're left wondering, "What's the deal?"

But then, autumn sweeps in, and everything kicks into high gear. Winter arrives, and you might find your motivation in hibernation. This ebb and flow are natural and truly beneficial for your business growth.

● ● ●

Consider how crops work: you plant in spring, bide your time through summer, reap your rewards in autumn, and then winter is your cue to rest before starting anew. It's unrealistic to expect a harvest season all year round. And this constant grind mindset?

It's like you're sowing seeds at every chance—spring, summer, fall, winter, repeat—until you hit a wall by the time spring comes back. You're drained and considering giving up without experiencing the full results of your labor. Remember, inspiration, creativity, and progress follow the natural rhythm of seasons and cycles. Embrace it. Personal affirmations have helped me during pressure-filled moments, especially when reflecting on my relentless past.

The more fun I have, the more I make. Start having fun in your business. The more relaxed I feel, the wealthier I get. Allow yourself to rest.

During a lull in their design business, Taylor embraced the slowdown as a creative hibernation period, focusing on skill enhancement and seeking inspiration without the pressure of constant productivity. This strategic pause bore fruit when an influx of projects emerged, reminiscent of a bountiful autumn, demonstrating the value of preparation during quieter times. Taylor learned the importance of aligning with life's rhythms, discovering that embracing periods of calm can lead to surges of success and that taking time for growth and rejuvenation is not only beneficial for personal well-being but also for business vitality.

Creatives might experience fluctuations in income, but by understanding and preparing for these cycles, they can stabilize their financial situation and attract consistent work.

12. The Law of Gender: *Masculine and Feminine Energies Exist in Nature and Must be Balanced*

Feminine energy is all about flowing, while masculine energy focuses on grinding. In the life cycle of your business, you'll oscillate between these two dynamics. There'll be moments for action and moments to just let things be. And who's aiming for their business to sustain them for decades upon decades, right?

It's crucial to strike a harmony between surrendering and acting because ten years of pure surrender leads nowhere, and ten years of non-stop action are unsustainable. There will be times when a burst of inspiration hits, and you'll find yourself effortlessly creating courses, drafting emails, or churning out posts.

You'll find joy in this creativity, fueled by inspiration. But don't worry, you won't remain trapped in this cycle forever. The passion to nurture your business is ingrained, ensuring that your motivation will renew itself over time.

Jamie launched an eco-friendly gear startup, embracing a relentless work ethic driven by a traditional push for achievement from the start. Recognizing the need for balance, Jamie shifted towards a more intuitive approach, blending periods of intense work with moments of reflection and natural inspiration. This balance became Jamie's strategy for maintaining creativity and ensuring sustainable growth, proving that success lies in harmonizing the drive for progress with the wisdom of patience.

By staying receptive, that wave of inspiration will inevitably return. It's about leveraging your intuition to discern when to lean into each energy, guided by your immediate inspirations. The sparks of creativity in your business serve as your spiritual compass. Maintain this vital connection and always heed the wisdom of your instincts.

Diving into those twelve universal laws of manifestation has been quite the journey, but what comes next? How do we implement these big ideas to work for us in the real world? It's all about shifting gears from that non-stop hustle to a vibe where manifesting and a chill money mindset take the lead. Some folks are already surfing this wave, making things happen in a big way, while others might still feel stuck in the old grind.

That old-school approach of just working harder and harder, like trying to grow a garden in the middle of winter, often leaves us feeling knocked around by stuff we can't control, like sudden changes in algorithms. It's a familiar rut, right? But here's the twist: we understand that what's happening inside us deeply influences what's happening outside. So, forget sweating the small stuff like ad costs shooting up; it's about spotting the silver linings and counting our wins.

We've all heard (or even believed) those tired myths: making it in the creative world is too tough, there's too much competition, or it's not a "real" job. But what if we flipped the script? See a hurdle? That's your cue to learn something new. Nailed a goal? Take a moment to give yourself a high five. This whole thing is about moving through life with a bit more ease and grace, always feeling guided by something bigger — call it your gut, the universe, whatever works for you. Letting success unfold is the name of the game.

Getting these laws to work for you can elevate your career, your business, and even your bank account in ways you've only dreamed of. Imagine if every doubt about your potential just vanished. It's time to kick those doubts to the curb and start playing a bigger game. Manifestation? It's about making sure your expectations and desires agree. Use your mindset as your secret weapon in your business game plan. Sure, keeping up with the latest strategies and learning new tricks is key, but aligning your mindset with your goals? That's the real fundamental change.

Oh, and one last note. Let's take a moment to chat about something that happens all too often when we dive into the world of universal laws. It's a bit like finding out there's an additional layer to reality, from the law of attraction to the principles of cause and effect, and it's exciting, right? But here's the thing: as we get more into it, we notice how everyone disagrees, and it's super tempting to point fingers or think we need to step in and show them the 'right' way.

Here's the twist, though: When we focus on where we think others are slipping up, we're truly stepping out of our own magic circle. It's kind of like when you're trying to stay on your diet, but you're too busy checking out what's on everyone else's plate. Our minds love distraction, especially when it's about others because it means we don't have to scrutinize our own stuff.

Getting caught up in what everyone else is doing wrong is missing the point. Sure, it might feel easier and entertaining to spotlight where others aren't making the grade, but that's not the true purpose of what we're here to do. Our major gig is to keep it real with ourselves, to stay true to our path, and to ask those big questions: How can I grow? How can I shift my path for the better? What steps can I take to pursue my wildest aspirations in life?

Each person has their own unique journey, and we can only have a limited understanding of someone else's path. Worrying about whether someone else is out of sync with the universal laws is a bit like worrying if someone else's shoes are tied properly. Not really our business, right?

So, the game plan is simple: keep your eyes on your own path. Dive deep into self-reflection, embrace your authentic self, and sprinkle a little kindness on yourself along the way. It's about making your journey as enriching and fulfilling as possible. After all, when you stay in your lane with love and kindness, that's when you truly thrive.

Chapter Takeaways:
- Cultivating a mindset of abundance and positivity can transform challenges into opportunities, leading to both personal fulfillment and professional success.
- Embracing periods of rest and reflection is as crucial as action, allowing for a more sustainable and inspired creative process.
- Integrating universal laws into daily practices empowers individuals to navigate life with greater intention, harmony, and effectiveness.

Action Step:

Choose an area of your life or business you wish to improve. Apply the Law of Inspired Action by planning and executing one small, concrete step towards that goal today.

3 Raising Your Vibrational Frequency

*"You hold the tuning fork to your vibrational frequency.
Strike it with gratitude, resonate with joy, and let the universe
harmonize with your highest intentions."*

JEN FONTANILLA

Our goal is to increase and sustain our frequency throughout the day. But why is this important? The Law of Attraction suggests that we attract what we resonate with. Basically, we are going to attract other people or things that are at the same frequency as ours.

And when we raise our frequency, we can attract and manifest people, opportunities, places, and events so much faster and with ease and flow. This is so important for us to do regardless of whatever is going on all around us each and every day.

The Science of Vibration

But have you ever thought about how everything around us, including ourselves, is kind of vibrating? Sounds a bit out there, right? Stick with me. This isn't just a wild idea; it's actually something that scientists, especially those brainy quantum physics folks, have been talking about for a while. At the heart of it, they're saying that at the tiniest levels, our universe is more about vibes than solid stuff. Everything is in motion all the time.

Now, before we go any further, let's talk about this thing called vibrational frequency charts. Think of it as a guide or a map that shows different energy or consciousness levels and their vibes, measured in MHz. It's fascinating because it categorizes everything from our emotions to our thoughts into different frequencies. For instance, lower vibes like fear and guilt have their own MHz, and higher vibes like love and enlightenment? Yep, they have their higher MHz. Visualize your position on the vibe spectrum and shift to higher frequencies.

THE EMOTIONAL VIBRATION FREQUENCY CHART

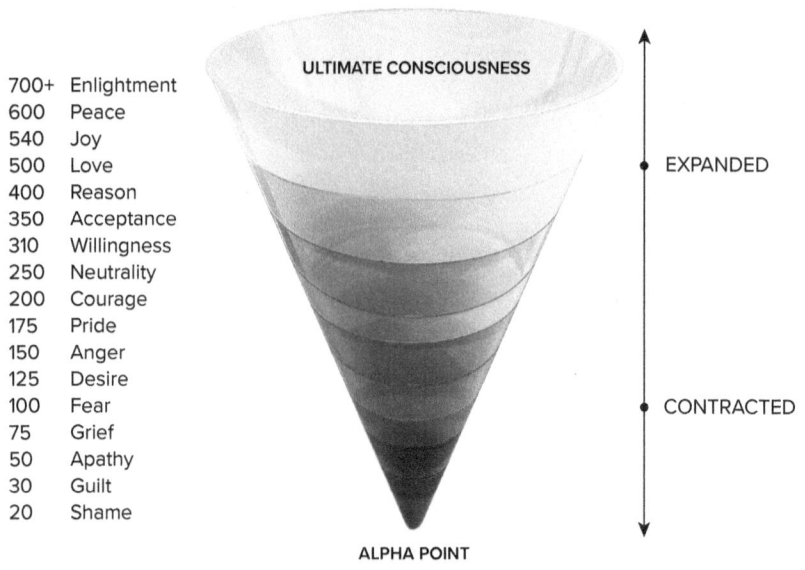

700+	Enlightment	
600	Peace	
540	Joy	
500	Love	EXPANDED
400	Reason	
350	Acceptance	
310	Willingness	
250	Neutrality	
200	Courage	
175	Pride	
150	Anger	
125	Desire	
100	Fear	CONTRACTED
75	Grief	
50	Apathy	
30	Guilt	
20	Shame	

ULTIMATE CONSCIOUSNESS

ALPHA POINT

Dr. David Hawkins, author of *Power vs. Force* and *Letting Go*, created a chart that assigns a numerical scale to common emotions. The chart is called the Emotional Vibration Analysis Frequency Chart and is based on Hawkins's work developing the Hawkins Scale of Consciousness, which measures emotions on a scale of 1 to 1000.

Now, you might wonder, "Who even figured this stuff out?" Niels Bohr, a Danish physicist who helped us understand a lot about how atoms work and how they're not just sitting still. There is also Dr. Masaru Emoto, who did some eye-opening experiments that suggested our thoughts and intentions might actually have the power to change the physical world around us.

Creativity and the Law of Attraction

Here's where it gets really interesting for us creative types. If everything has its own vibe, that means we're all putting out our own frequencies based on how we feel, what we think, and how we're doing in life. Ever heard of the Law of Attraction? It's this idea that like attracts like. So, if you're vibing high, feeling good, and thinking positive, you're more likely to attract good stuff into your life, including creative inspiration and, yes, even money.

But why does this matter for creatives? Well, think about it. Creativity is a positive frequency. When you're in that creative flow, you're in tune with the best vibes. And the cool part? This high vibe can help pull in opportunities, make your work resonate more with others, and yes, even help you attract some cash. It's like tuning into your favorite radio station and finding out they're giving away free concert tickets—you just have to be on the right frequency.

The Inner Work for Higher Frequency

So, how do you get onto that frequency? It's all about doing the inner work. I'm talking about dealing with your baggage, setting some solid boundaries, and getting rid of any negative energy that's dragging you down. It's about getting to a place where you love yourself and feel worthy of success and creativity. Cleaning house internally creates space for positive opportunities to find you.

Understanding vibrational frequency can be life-changing for creative individuals. Understanding and working with universal laws unlocks creativity and opportunities. And let's be real, who wouldn't want that?

Understanding Vibrational Energy

Let's dive into the fascinating world where science meets the essence of our being. Picture this: at the core of everything you see, touch, taste, and feel are tiny, buzzing particles called atoms. It's like we're all made of LEGO blocks but made of pure energy instead of plastic. This isn't just poetic musings; it's quantum physics, showing us the universe's building blocks and how fundamentally, we're all connected through this vibrant energy field.

Atoms themselves are fascinating creatures. They are mostly empty space with a nucleus at the center. Atoms never actually touch anything, which is mind-blowing. The sensations we interpret as touch or physical contact are just electromagnetic forces repelling each other. So, when you tap your phone screen or hug a friend, it's a dance of electromagnetic fields and forces, not direct contact.

Now, zooming out from the atomic level, everything you see around you – from the coffee cup on your desk to the trees outside your window – is made up of these atoms vibrating at different frequencies. This vibration is where the magic happens. It's why a piece of metal feels solid and cold, water flows, and air is invisible. They're all made of the same building blocks, just dancing to different tunes.

Bringing it back to us, humans, our bodies are buzzing cities of atoms, constantly in motion, vibrating, exchanging energy with everything around us. This exchange is what keeps us alive and connected to the world. Our thoughts, emotions, and physical health are all expressions of these vibrational frequencies. Ever walked into a room and felt the mood without anyone saying a word? That's you, tuning into the vibrational energy of the place.

In essence, understanding that we're made of energy and atoms helps us grasp our profound connection to the universe and each other. It's a reminder that at our core, we're all just star stuff, vibrating away, creating this beautiful symphony of existence. So, next time you feel isolated or disconnected, remember that you're literally a part of everything, connected at the atomic level to the cosmos.

Navigation Emotional Frequencies

Understanding frequencies is like understanding our emotional states.

Picture yourself in front of an old-school radio with a manual dial. When you dial it to 95.5 FM, you catch the tunes playing on that frequency. Switch the dial and vibe to a different genre on another station. Different music genres are broadcasted on multiple stations at the same time. It's the radio's job to tune into the specific frequency of the music you want to hear.

This scenario reflects our existence and operation. Like a radio, we're constantly surrounded by emotional frequencies. Our personal tuner—our emotional state—determines which frequency we're attuned to. Feeling upbeat and energetic? You're tuned into a frequency vibrating with joy. Feeling down or anxious? Your dial is tuned to a lower frequency, matching those emotions.

Remember the visual of the radio with that little orange indicator moving across the dial? That's like asking yourself, "How do I feel right now?" Our emotions indicate our current frequency. Instead of frequencies being numbers like on the radio dial, we describe them with words that represent our emotional states.

The emotional spectrum is huge, stretching from low-frequency feelings like depression through mid-range emotions like contentment to high-frequency states described as joy or bliss—emotions so profound they're often beyond words. Just as a radio tuner allows us to select the music we wish to listen to, our awareness and choices can shift our emotional "frequency." By understanding this, we can more consciously navigate our emotional landscape, tuning into the vibes that elevate us and those around us.

Releasing Negative Frequencies

Imagine this: you're driving your kid to basketball practice, and out of nowhere, someone cuts you off. "Are you serious?! You've got to be kidding me!" You might scream as waves of anger and frustration crash over you. It's in moments like these that we often pick up little rocks of anger and tuck them into our metaphorical backpacks. These rocks vary in size—some are hefty boulders, while others are mere pebbles.

Now, picture trying to scale a mountain, say Mount Everest, with this backpack loaded with stones of negativity. It's an uphill struggle. It is essential to let go of negative emotions. Our goal is to keep our emotional backpack as light as possible, tuning into higher frequencies of positivity and joy.

The key here isn't just about occasional self-care during a five-minute morning routine. It's about constantly being aware of how we feel throughout the day. Each moment we choose to hold onto a rock of anger, we're choosing to weigh down our backpack further. Learning to let go of these rocks, to not stash them away for 'safekeeping,' is crucial. Releasing burdens helps us climb personal mountains with ease and stay tuned to higher vibrations.

Elevating Our Vibrational Frequency

But how do we boost our frequency, especially when we feel like we're operating on a lower wavelength than we'd prefer? Your main focus needs to be prioritizing your highest vibrational frequency.

But let's broaden our perspective a bit. Think of raising your frequency not just as a mood boost but as an expansion of your consciousness. It's about transitioning from a state of lower awareness to one of heightened perception. And here's the cool part: as we climb higher on this ladder of consciousness, we unlock the gates for our intuition to run wild and free.

Elevating our frequency, therefore, becomes a journey of self-discovery, where increasing our level of consciousness can lead to a more intuitive, aligned, and harmonious existence. This isn't just about feeling good; it's about tapping into a deeper, more profound aspect of our being. Lower-frequency vibes block our inner wisdom and gut feelings.

Abraham Hicks and the Natural State of Being

Abraham Hicks represents the teachings of Esther Hicks and the collective consciousness known as Abraham. These teachings focus on the Law of Attraction and the power of vibration in shaping our lives.

Abraham Hicks uses a captivating analogy: the cork in water. Visualize a cork effortlessly floating on water. Its natural state is to float, to bob along the surface without a care in the world. This, according to Abraham Hicks, is akin to our own natural state of being – one of ease, floating atop life's vibrational waves.

This may be hard to accept, especially if you're going through a difficult time. The key takeaway is not about striving to improve ourselves as if we are flawed. Rather, it's about realizing that it's us – yes, us – who are often the ones pushing the cork underwater, holding ourselves back from rising.

Picture yourself holding a submerged cork. It naturally rises to the top when released. This simple act of letting go is pivotal in the journey to align with our highest vibrational state. It's about releasing those emotions that weigh us down, those that do not serve our highest good. Letting go isn't just a step in the process; it's the essence of the process, allowing us to return to our natural state of buoyancy and joy, much like the cork destined to float.

Mastering Our Emotional Frequency

Our emotions are like dashboard lights indicating our frequency. But where do these emotions come from? It all starts with our thoughts. That's right, our thoughts set the stage for our feelings, sparking a feedback loop where emotions fuel more thoughts, which can lead to a not-so-fun merry-go-round of negativity. Picture this: someone drops a not-so-nice comment on your Facebook post, and suddenly, you're swimming in a sea of anger, hurt, or maybe feeling a bit exposed.

Here's a game-changer, though: that comment isn't the direct cause of your emotional storm. If we thought that, we'd feel pretty helpless, right? The real power move is realizing we've got the control and the choice—yep, it's all about snapping out of autopilot and deciding how we want to feel moment by moment. The true culprit behind the curtain? It's the thoughts we entertain about that comment. It's how we interpret it, how we let it define us, that stirs the pot.

Often, we mesh together the comment and our reaction, thinking, "That comment wrecked my day." But in reality, it's not the comment pulling the strings—it's us. We might jump to conclusions like, "If this person thinks this way about me, everyone must!" or "There goes my business down the drain!" Believing those thoughts can indeed make everything feel pretty lousy.

And once you're in that lousy headspace, guess what? The Law of Attraction attracts more negativity, spiraling you into a negative vibe vortex. So, the real deal here is learning to be a master of where we point our mental spotlight. Choose uplifting thoughts instead of burdensome ones. This is all about choosing thoughts that make us feel good, breaking free from the cycle, and steering our emotional ship toward brighter waters.

Gratitude: The Ultimate Vibration Enhancer

Envision your hand accidentally coming into contact with a flame. Ouch, right? Instinctively, just like you, I'd yank my hand back. Similarly, when we encounter something in our lives or business that stings, the smart move is to pull back. This isn't just about physical space but mentally shifting gears away from those scorching thoughts that can burn us.

It's crucial to direct our thoughts and focus on what feels more soothing, more positive. Wondering how to make that shift toward the good stuff? One of the most powerful tools I've discovered, and something I lean on heavily in my own life, is the practice of gratitude. It's like the ultimate vibe shifter. Gratitude has this incredible way of recalibrating our emotional state. It's quite fascinating how quickly it can move us from a place of negativity to a more balanced, thankful state.

Abraham often mentions how tough it can be to jump from deep sadness to outright joy. But gratitude? That's accessible from almost any emotional place we find ourselves in. It acts as a gentle bridge to uplifted feelings.

Jumping straight from feeling down to over-the-moon happy? Yeah, that's a tough leap. But guess what? No matter where you're at, there's always something to be thankful for. Ever catch yourself eyeing someone else's progress, thinking, "Wow, they've got it all figured out," and then feeling a bit rubbish about where you're at? Here's a newsflash: it's not their achievements making you feel low. It's the story you're telling yourself about what their success means for you.

What if, instead, we flipped the script and found joy in their achievements? Imagine thinking, "Hey, it's awesome to see someone killing it. It means I can do it too!" Suddenly, the vibe shifts. Seeing others succeed becomes proof that you're just as capable. That shift in perspective? It feels fantastic.

The game plan to increase your vibe: quit hurting yourself. Focus on the stuff that makes you feel stellar. First, genuinely care about your feelings. Hit a rough patch? Dive in and ask, "What's bumming me out?" More often than not, it's because you've locked your sights on something that's as pleasant as a hand in a flame. Time to shift your focus to what feels right.

And here's a little wisdom nugget I picked up: keep a mental (or physical) list of your feel-good go-tos. Whether it's a song that never fails to uplift you, a heartwarming memory, or just stepping outside for fresh air—knowing what lifts you up can be a game-changer.

Aligning with Higher Frequencies

It's not about forcing something that doesn't fit when things get tricky. It's not about amping up the struggle or showcasing how hard we can make it for ourselves. Clearly, that's a no-go if we're aiming for good vibes.

When things get tough, we need to pause, step back, and raise our frequency. That's when the magic happens—opportunities, clarity, and ideas start flowing in. That's what alignment feels like.

Here are a few things we can do to raise our frequency:

- **Be Around Other Amazing People**

  Being around incredible people naturally lifts your spirits. Being with your closest friends or people you admire feels awesome, doesn't it? Sure, not everyone's going to say, "Hanging with my friends is the best!" but being in the company of those who inspire you, those you look up to, has this way of making everything seem brighter.

  The same thing happens when you go to a conference with like-minded people, and you're left feeling like your brain is on fire (in a good way!) with ideas. Your frequency is increasing due to the positive energy around you. And it's not just a one-way street; it's like a group lift where everyone's vibes are soaring.

  So, if you're stuck, get around some incredible like-minded, inspirational individuals, even for a bit, because it can work wonders. Give it a go. Before you realize it, new insights will flood your mind. That's the power of surrounding yourself with amazing people.

- **Play the Power of Music**

  Music is like our personal vibe guide because, at its core, it's all about frequency. And the cool part? You can dial into music anytime, anywhere. Personally, I love starting off my mornings with some music in the background while I'm journaling or doing my Morning Pages.

Do you ever notice how we all plug into our favorite playlists at the gym or when going for a run? Music has the ability to energize and transform our moods rapidly.

Now, here's a little trick I've been onto for a while, and you're gonna want to try this. Hit up YouTube and look up 528 Hertz. You'll find a goldmine of tracks to explore. I've had this frequency playing in the background for hours while I work. They say it's the heartbeat of the universe's musical matrix – pretty crazy, right? It's like tuning into the frequency of love, which, if you think about it, is pretty much what we're all about.

So, what's our end goal? To vibe on that level of unconditional love as much as we can, all day, every day. Sure, it's a tall order when you're gritting your teeth in traffic or getting frustrated waiting for your food order that's already taking too long, but this frequency, it's got something special. They say it can even help fix our DNA, which sounds like a stretch until you try it and feel the difference. Give it a try and see how it changes things for you.

- **Embracing the Great Outdoors: Nature and Movement**
There's something magical about taking a daily stroll through the grass and wandering around a botanical garden. It's not just about soaking in the beauty of nature; it also gets me moving. And moving is key—think of it as the next chapter in our quest for a higher vibe. Exercise not only releases endorphins but also provides additional benefits. As humans, we're built to move. Our bodies weren't made for staring at screens all day.

Ever experienced that euphoria known as a runner's high? That's what I'm talking about. Whether it's a leisurely jog or an all-out sprint, finishing feels incredible, thanks to a rush of endorphins. It's a natural boost that reminds us of the joy of being active.

- **Finding Your Joy: Engage in What Lights You Up**

Discovering activities that spark a genuine sense of joy is like uncovering treasure. It's about gravitating towards things that lift your spirits and fill you with energy. Immerse yourself in experiences that resonate deeply with you.

Engaging with what inspires you isn't just a pastime; it's a vital part of maintaining your vibrational frequency. Focusing on what brings you joy enriches your life and strengthens your connection to your inner self. It's like tuning your radio to the best station possible—one that plays your favorite songs, one after another.

So, take a moment to explore. Reflect on what brings you the most happiness and contentment. Is it creating something with your hands? Is it the thrill of learning something new? Maybe it's the simple pleasure of watching the sunrise. Whatever it is, make space for it in your life. By doing so, you're not only nurturing your soul but also inviting more positivity and light into every day.

- **Cultivating Joy: The Art of Appreciation and Gratitude**

Ever wonder how some people seem to attract positivity like magnets? The secret might just lie in the power of gratitude and appreciation. Exploring these practices can greatly impact our interaction with the world, boosting our vibrational frequency. But why is gratitude so transformative? It's because gratitude resonates with the energy of abundance and receiving. It promotes contentment and reduces cravings or feelings of lack.

What if gratitude meant being content and happy, regardless of circumstances? Imagine the freedom and peace that come from this absolute detachment. Could this be the key to attracting even more positivity into our lives?

By recognizing and appreciating the good in our lives, we attract more blessings. This approach not only enhances our daily experience but also encourages a flow of even more reasons to be grateful. It's worth exploring how this positive feedback loop can unfold in our lives with just a shift towards more gratitude.

The Power of Letting Go and Forgiveness

Ever watch a toddler in their natural habitat? Take my cousin's little two-year-old daughter, for example. The kid's a bundle of joy, bouncing around without a care in the world. It's not like she's been hitting the books, learning how to crank up her happiness levels. No way. She's living her best life, just being naturally happy. Pure, unfiltered joy—that's our factory setting.

Somewhere along the way, we picked up this habit of dialing down our vibes. And you know what? A lot of it comes down to the baggage we insist on carrying around. Our past hang-ups can weigh us down, making it difficult to feel good.

If you're sitting there thinking, "Ugh, feeling blissed out all the time feels like a stretch," I get it. It's probably because there's something you're clutching onto pretty tightly. I'm right there with you; letting go isn't always easy. It's like you start off holding a tiny pebble of a grudge or regret, and before you know it, you're lugging around a whole backpack full of rocks and maybe even a bowling ball or two. Carrying all that makes it tough to lift your spirits and boost your vibe.

Release and Forgive: Clearing the Path to Joy

Now, here's a sneak peek into what's coming up: we're going to get into releasing and forgiving. (Did you just cringe?) And let me tell you, this is huge. It's not just about dropping those rocks; it's about rediscovering that joyful, carefree vibe we were all born with. Getting there might require a bit of willingness to let go and step away from that learned helplessness, release those emotions, and embrace the desire to feel lighter.

Embracing Lightness: A Journey Back to Joy

We clear emotional clutter by letting go and forgiving. This makes room for higher vibrational frequencies to take root. Imagine your mind as a garden. It may have been overrun with weeds, symbolizing grudges, regrets, and pains. Starting the cleanup might seem daunting at first, but as you pull each weed and plant new seeds, you'll begin to see a transformation. Your mind blooms with joy, peace, and love.

This journey back to joy isn't about ignoring the real pains and challenges of life. It's about choosing not to let them define our entire existence. It's about acknowledging our pain, learning from our experiences, and then gently, but firmly, deciding to move forward. It's understanding that We are

• • •

responsible for our vibrational frequency and can align it with joy, love, and abundance.

Daily Practices for Higher Vibration

To maintain this higher frequency, consider integrating daily practices that reinforce positive vibes. This could be anything from meditation, which helps center your thoughts and emotions, to practicing mindfulness throughout your day, ensuring that you're fully present and appreciating each moment. Incorporating affirmations can also be powerful, helping to rewire your subconscious mind toward positivity and abundance.

When in a bad space, I ask myself: How long do I want to stay here? And when, of course, I realize the answer is, "I don't at all," it will shift the way I feel. I also visualize that vibrational frequency chart in my mind, and I imagine giving myself a score and if I am at the bottom of that funnel, I ask myself, "Where do you want to move up to? At times, I'm not mentally prepared to jump to the top of the funnel. But if I can even just move a few levels up, I am already setting myself up to feeling better.

Remember, the journey to a higher vibrational frequency is a continuous process, filled with learning, growth, and, most importantly, gentle self-compassion. Celebrate your victories, no matter how small, and always be kind to yourself along the way. After all, it's not just about the destination but the transformation and growth that happen within us as we make this journey.

Chapter Takeaways:

- Embracing vibrational energy: Acknowledge the vibrational nature of everything, including ourselves, to grasp our interconnectedness and place in the universe.

- Letting go for lightness: Releasing negative emotions is essential for maintaining emotional lightness and attracting positive experiences into our lives.

- Inner growth for higher frequencies: Prioritize inner work and self-love to create room for elevated vibrational experiences and opportunities.

Action Step:

Embrace a daily practice of acknowledging three things you're grateful for, allowing this habit to become a beacon that guides you towards positivity, peace, and a profound connection with the abundance around you. This practice is not just about identifying the good in your life but about feeling it deeply, setting the foundation for a life vibrated at a frequency of joy, love, and endless possibilities. Let this be your first step on a path that transforms not just your mindset but your entire existence.

BONUS MATERIAL

The **"HIGHER SELF MEDITATION"** is your key to unlocking creative potential and embracing your higher self. Immerse yourself in this guided journey twice daily to elevate your vibrational frequency, foster intuition, and manifest abundance.

JUST SCAN THE QR CODE RIGHT HERE OR VISIT THE LINK BELOW TO ACCESS YOUR FREE BONUS!

SCAN ME

www.jenmoneycoach.com/the-creative-code-book-bonuses

● ● ●

4 Taking Inventory

"In the willingness to face our financial truths,
we find the power to transform our realities."

JEN FONTANILLA

Whether we make our own money or rely on someone else, many of us would rather pretend our financial matters don't exist, or we hope they'll just take care of themselves somehow. Why do we prefer not to look at reality? Our financial problems are overwhelming. We wear metaphorical blinders to avoid being blinded. We continue to live our lives automatically, perpetuating the same pattern today in and day out. After all, confronting our money issues forces us to confront our feelings of self-worth or lack thereof. So, we stay in the same old situations because we're comforted by the familiar, even if the familiar is terrible. Unconsciously, we avoid situations involving financial problems. We can look at the state of our self-worth by looking at our net worth, and in order to improve this, the first step is to take off the blinders and look at what you've been hiding from.

Let's embark on an exercise that puts everything on the table.

1. Write down all of your complaints about money. What drives you crazy? What do you absolutely loathe?

2. What are the daily problems you face with money?

3. Who or what is obstructing your path to financial comfort? Put everything out there—no restrictions.

4. What aspects of your finances do you prefer not to think about? What makes you want to look away or flee?

5. Once you've got all that down, take a deep breath. There it is… the raw truth about your financial frustrations. What you may have convinced yourself was inevitable is not your destiny. You're poised to start transforming it immediately. Hold onto this list; we'll return to it.

6. Inscribe these words at the bottom of your page: *"My new life of high self-worth, high net worth, and financial ease begins now."* With that, your intention is set. Let's proceed.

Setting an intention is crucial - it propels us toward our true desires. Yet, this doesn't mean we can afford to bury our heads in the sand. If we're aiming to transform our financial landscape, avoiding the issue won't cut it. Ignoring our financial matters comes with its price. It might Dodging them now may seem simple, but it complicates things later. And let's be honest, that's not the future you envisioned when you set your intention!

You've already noted down the financial challenges you're facing. Now, it's time to dig deeper into the areas you might be avoiding. Identifying and confronting these avoidance patterns is the first step toward navigating toward a brighter, more secure future.

Let's Take Inventory of Your Habits and Patterns

This compilation highlights typical negative financial habits and tendencies, especially relevant for creatives like us. It's designed to illuminate areas where you've chosen not to see, opting instead for avoidance.

Grab your journal, or open up your computer, and carefully go through the statements below. Jot down those that resonate or mark them with a star or a circle.

By the end, you'll have identified your unique financial behaviors. For the moment, simply keep this list safe. There's no immediate action required on your part just yet.

1. I frequently find myself broke before all my bills are paid.
2. I tend to carry a persistent debt on my credit cards.
3. Reviewing or balancing my bank statements is something I avoid.
4. Examining my credit card statements isn't part of my routine.
5. The interest rates being applied to my accounts are a mystery to me.
6. A savings account is something I haven't set up.
7. Planning for retirement through an account has not been one of my actions.
8. Although I own a retirement account, making regular contributions isn't my habit.
9. The amount of money I spend on a regular basis is unknown to me.
10. Adherence is crucial for a meaningful financial plan.
11. Late payment charges are a frequent nuisance in my financial life.
12. Procrastination has become my approach to bill payments.

13. Overdraft fees from my bank are an all-too-common surprise.

14. Checking my credit report is a task I rarely, if ever, undertake.

15. My credit score remains an enigma to me.

16. Uncertainty about owing back taxes or being in debt to the IRS looms over me.

17. Personal financial resources are utterly nonexistent for me.

18. I haven't been in the workforce for ages.

19. Marketable skills are assets I find myself devoid of.

20. I am not knowledgeable about our financial situation.

21. My spouse or partner has taken on full responsibility for managing our finances.

22. The financial value I possess is a figure I'm oblivious to.

23. Absent from my documents are a will or any plans for estate management.

24. The financial aftermath of something happening to my spouse or partner is a scenario I'm unprepared for.

25. Shopping serves as an uncontrollable urge for me.

26. Dread of financial ruin outweighs fear of spending.

27. No matter the effort, financial sufficiency seems like an unattainable state.

28. Spending guilt plagues me since I am not the earner.

29. My tendency is to undervalue my products or services, often giving them away for minimal returns.

30. I struggle with setting appropriate prices.

31. The courage to request a raise or promotion escapes me.

32. Finding joy in my current employment is a challenge.

33. I crave a new career direction.

34. Clarity on my professional desires is absent.

• • •

35. Dependence on others for financial security has been a constant in my life.

36. I don't have the skillset for independent financial management.

37. Money quickly disappearing is a recurring theme for me.

38. Investing in others over myself has become a pattern.

39. Indulging in unaffordable luxuries is a guilty pleasure.

40. Financial support or loans from others have become a necessity for my survival.

41. My spending often extends to buying things on a whim that I later regret.

42. Investing in stocks or other financial instruments seems like a foreign concept to me.

43. I find it difficult to grasp the complexities of taxes and their effect on my income.

44. Negotiating salaries is a situation I find intimidating.

45. Keeping up with financial news or market trends is not part of my routine.

46. The concept of an emergency fund is something I'm not familiar with.

47. My living expenses often exceed my income.

48. Using money to solve problems or relieve stress is a habit I've developed.

49. Investing in personal development or education financially seems unaffordable to me.

50. The thought of tracking expenses through apps or spreadsheets is daunting and hence avoided.

If you want to add your own statements, you can.

Don't criticize yourself if you exceed your intended number of copies, circles, or stars. Engaging in this process changes your financial habits. You're already on the path to change.

We often avoid facing the truth about our financial situation. In the next part of this chapter, we're going to dive into some of the biggies. Guilt tops the list, and it's a massive one, especially for women!

Both men and women experience money guilt, but women feel it more. Research tells us ladies are not as quick to negotiate our salaries or ask for that well-deserved raise. And if we do ask and hear that the budget's tight, we're kinda prone to just back down, feeling bad for even bringing it up. Guys, though? They're more likely to stick it out and keep at it until they snag what they're after. For whatever reason, us women deal with self-worth issues that really show up when it comes to our finances, and too often, we end up just burying our heads in the sand about it.

Women often prioritize others over themselves and feel guilty about indulging in personal expenses. No one's a fan of feeling guilty, right? So, we end up doing whatever we can to sidestep those feelings - even if it means ignoring our own needs and wants.

But hey, as much as we love taking care of others, keeping the give and take in harmony is key if we're aiming for a good relationship with both ourselves and our bank accounts. With a solid sense of self-worth, we can look after ourselves just as fabulously as we do everyone else. And the best part? No guilt necessary. So, it's time to take those blinders off.

Then there's this idea some of us have that if we're rolling in it, it means someone else is missing out. It makes us feel bad for having plenty. But spiritual folks and even brainy types like Einstein have been saying for ages that everything, including money, is just energy. And since energy is always floating around (It doesn't disappear. It just transforms.), there's no cap on financial good fortune. Abundance is endless, folks.

Scared of How Awesome We Could Be

There's this tricky thing about avoiding the truth, especially when it's something we don't even realize we're doing. What if the stories we tell ourselves about money were fiction? What if we're destined for unlimited financial success? Many self-deprecating stories would crumble if that were true. We'd need to stretch beyond our comfort zones and stop selling ourselves short.

Do you ever dial it back for the sake of others? Holding back to stay loyal to those old, worn-out beliefs?

Take my buddy Angela, for example. She undervalues her stunning handmade clutches despite willing customers. The fear of taking the money arose from the uncertainty of finding buyers. Her self-worth issues made her unable to see the value of the clutches she was giving away.

Stepping into our power means kicking the habit of playing it safe. It starts with small steps but eventually leads to big leaps – changing jobs, shifting relationships, and chasing dreams. Growing into new versions of ourselves comes with a ton of uncertainty. To dodge this discomfort and fit in, we cling to cultural norms and the paths we've been told will make us happy. It's easier, right? No need to blaze new trails. We can just stay snug in the roles of daughter, son, wife, husband, mother, or father, avoiding the tough talks that come with challenging what everyone expects from us.

But really, how safe are those roles we cling to? How secure is it to live in little boxes and lead inauthentic lives? How damaging is it to undermine ourselves and reinforce the notion that we have little value?

The beliefs we hold about money—and our own value—lock us into less-than-fulfilling situations. They cage us in a fear of the unknown, where we're too scared to break out of our comfort zones. The real heartbreaker? We settle for less and miss out on the amazing lives we have.

I know when I have done this inventory checklist for myself at different stages of my journey, even in recent years, it can be very humbling, but I chose to give myself a lot of grace and remind myself that I am taking action, focusing on how, now that I am aware of what is happening, what small steps can I take to fix whatever is happening right now? Even just aiming for 1% better each week is going to get you further than being worried or afraid and never starting.

I'm here to challenge you to embrace change.

Here's the uplifting bit: We all have boundless potential. Our abilities can amaze us if fully utilized. Imagine that! Adopting an infinite mindset

• • •

towards money and self-worth begins the moment we remove our blinders and start acknowledging the areas where we've kept ourselves in the shadows.

Squaring Up with Your Financial Feels

When we splurge, hoard our cash, or turn a blind eye to our bank statements, we're actually dodging our emotions. Let's make it clear, our feelings are deeply intertwined with this money situation.

There are emotions we're all about embracing – joy, gratitude, love, thrill. But then there are those emotions we'd rather not acknowledge. Whatever we're ignoring, it's usually tangled up with those "I'd rather not deal with this" vibes.

Remember, you're not your emotions. They're just temporary guests, popping by for a visit before moving on. Allowing them their moment in your consciousness clears the way for happier, more welcome feelings to come through. Essentially, letting yourself feel the tough stuff opens you up to the joy when it knocks on your door.

A big part of the struggle is confronting how our reluctance to face the truth ties back to our sense of worthiness.

Later on, we'll dive into how tools like visualization, meditation, and the art of forgiveness can guide us through these murky waters, helping us let go of these heavy emotions and feelings of unworthiness. Removing the old creates space for our genuine desires.

Chapter Takeaways:

- Confronting financial blind spots: Acknowledge and confront financial challenges to initiate improvement.

- Setting intentions and facing reality: Intentions are crucial but must align with facing financial truths to avoid complications later.

- Overcoming Guilt and Self-Worth Issues: Combat guilt and self-worth issues, especially among women, for financial empowerment.

- Embracing Potential and Confronting Emotions: Challenge limiting beliefs and confront emotions to unlock boundless potential and invite positive change.

Action Step:

Schedule a "Money Date" with yourself. Set aside 30 minutes this week to sit down in a quiet, comfortable space with your financial statements. Bring your bank statements, credit card statements, and any bills or financial obligations you have. Use this time to simply review and acknowledge your current financial situation without judgment or action. Just observe and take note of your thoughts and feelings as you go through the documents. This is your first step towards financial awareness and honesty with yourself.

5 Uncovering Your Money Stories and Transforming Them

*"Every decision you make writes a line in the story
of your financial life. Choose the ones that lead you
to the chapters filled with fulfillment and prosperity."*

JEN FONTANILLA

I sat there in the corner of my childhood bedroom, holding the broken pieces of mylar from the popped helium balloon. Tears began to stream down my flushed cheeks as soon as I realized what I had just done.

During our visit to the local mall, I was filled with excitement as a four-year-old when I came across a balloon person offering an incredible variety of character helium balloons. Like any girl growing up in the early eighties, I had an absolute obsession with Strawberry Shortcake. However, my dad went to buy one for me, but when he returned, it wasn't Strawberry Shortcake. It was Wonder Woman. My heart sank from disappointment, and rather than be grateful, I sat in silence on the ride back, thinking of how this wasn't the balloon I wanted.

As soon as we got back home, I found a safety pin and popped it. The tear in the balloon grew, causing it to rapidly lose air as it deflated. It was then that I recalled my first moment of shame and sadness because my parents' hard-earned money was wasted on me. I realized that I had acted like an ungrateful brat and there was nothing I could do to make the balloon whole again.

And since then, it has always been hard to ask for any kind of gift because the feeling that I don't deserve it is firmly engrained in me. Even now, remembering that moment makes me cry because it reminds me of how I squandered that gift.

Your money mindset influences how you handle and feel about cash. Understanding this helps you see why building a positive outlook towards money is super important for getting your finances on the up and up.

Right at the core of how we deal with our finances is our money mindset, which is this intricate system shaped by all sorts of beliefs about money. T. Harv Eker points out in "Secrets of the Millionaire Mind" that it's not just a bunch of random thoughts jumbled together, but rather a well-organized setup that really dictates our financial future.

This framework shapes your financial interactions through a sequential process:

1. The beliefs and thoughts you hold shape your emotional responses.
2. These emotions guide your decision-making process and actions.
3. Finally, your actions influence your financial outcomes and wealth.

So, this programming nudges you into forming certain habits and acting in particular ways that bring about outcomes that match up with your money mindset.

Unpacking Money Beliefs

Grasping the origins of your money beliefs, how they shape your ease with finances, and the challenges they pose to bettering your financial state is crucial. You didn't intentionally choose these money beliefs - you may not even be fully aware of them. Even if you believe your views on money are positive, it's likely there are some contradictions in there. That's because these beliefs weren't consciously selected; instead, as you grew up, you soaked up the money beliefs from those around you without even realizing it.

Take this scenario: If your folks always seemed to be hustling yet could hardly afford the fun stuff, you might end up thinking, "No matter how hard I try, I just can't make enough money to enjoy life."

If you grew up with financial security, you might believe you will always have what you need.

Your beliefs reflect your early experiences. Your upbringing influences your money mindset, but you can shape your own beliefs.

No matter the scenario, how you perceived your early years shaped your money beliefs and how you handle finances today. If you aligned with the way you were raised, you probably adopted the financial viewpoints of your main influences (often your parents). This has steered your money mindset to mimic those early examples.

If you're familiar with your parents struggling financially, you may face similar challenges. Conversely, if they were adept at managing their

● ● ●

finances, you're likely more confident with your money. However, if you rejected the lessons from your upbringing, you might have developed a money mindset that challenges those early examples.

For instance, if you grew up witnessing financial hardship, you might now be driven to achieve wealth and indulge in the finer things in life. Alternatively, if you came from a wealthy background but felt neglected, you might now associate money with negative emotions, making financial matters uncomfortable for you.

Your personal experiences with money during your formative years play a significant role in shaping your beliefs. Say your family couldn't afford something you wanted; you might have felt grateful for their effort, or possibly upset and let down by their inability to meet your desires. These reactions contribute to the development of your financial beliefs and behaviors.

Establishing Financial Comfort Zones

The emotions you felt led to specific beliefs forming in your mind. These beliefs shape how comfortable you feel with money. Essentially, your money mindset also decides how much money you believe you can handle or manage well.

Let's call this your financial comfort zone. It's like your money mindset has set up rules for how you think and act around money, sticking closely to this comfort zone. If you somehow make or save more than this comfort zone allows, hanging onto it becomes tough. That's because, deep down, your mindset is convinced you're not cut out for the bigger financial leagues. It reminds me of how many lottery winners blow through their jackpot only to find themselves broke again in just a few years. In fact, stats show that about one-third of lottery winners go bankrupt in three to five years, a rate higher than that of the average American, as pointed out by the Certified Financial Planner Board of Standards.

Financial comfort zones explain why the cycle of poverty persists for some and wealth remains constant for others. Everyone has a unique threshold for the amount of money they're at ease handling – for some, it's just a small sum, while for others, it can be millions.

If you find it hard to make more money or save it, it's likely due to the limiting beliefs you've adopted, which cap your financial threshold.

The Role of Limiting Beliefs
Limiting beliefs are defense mechanisms, as Maltz explains in "Psycho Cybernetics." Identifying too closely with a distressing event can lead to negative emotions. In response, you concluded what caused the discomfort and vowed to avoid similar situations in the future to shield yourself from the pain.

This decision then solidified into a subconscious belief that influences how you think, feel, and act, even if you're not aware of it. For instance, if your parents worked tirelessly but never spent on themselves, giving away any surplus to relatives who asked, you might have grown to resent both the relatives for taking advantage and your parents for not prioritizing their own needs. This could lead you to equate having money with vulnerability to exploitation, convincing yourself it's better not to accumulate wealth than to risk being used.

Such a belief sets a financial ceiling for yourself, convincing you it's safer to stay below a certain wealth threshold to avoid being taken advantage of. This example shows how deep-seated, disempowering beliefs can anchor you below your potential financial level.

Let's explore three ways such limiting beliefs can block your path to financial success.

- **First, they trap you in a victim mindset.** These beliefs lead you to think you're powerless over your financial future, causing you to dodge full accountability for your finances. This avoidance means you might not see how your own choices and actions have landed you where you are. Stuck in this mindset, you miss out on learning from past errors and grabbing new opportunities, gradually eating away at your self-esteem and cementing the false idea that you're not capable of better financial management.

- **Second, they coax you into justifying your financial scarcity.** Self-doubt about wealth makes you believe it's not important or too difficult to acquire. Excuses hinder growth and keep you in your comfort zone.

- **Lastly, they saddle you with guilt over wealth.** Believing that wanting or having money is morally incorrect can lead to guilt when desiring more. This internal conflict can paralyze you, making you shy away from opportunities to increase your wealth, fearing that pursuing more money makes you a bad person.

Into the World of Money Stories

As we transition from discussing the broad impact of our money mindset on our financial behaviors and outcomes, we move toward the concept of money stories. These narratives are deeply personal accounts of our financial lives, crafted from our own experiences, beliefs, and emotions about money. While our mindset forms the foundation of our financial attitudes and actions, our money stories add depth and detail, painting a fuller picture of our relationship with money. Turning our attention from the overarching themes of money mindsets, we'll now explore the unique and compelling stories that reveal the individual paths we navigate in our financial worlds.

Stepping away from the tight grip of limiting beliefs about money, let's ease into something a bit more personal: our money stories. These aren't just about how much cash we have in the bank; they're the unique, sometimes messy tales of our financial lives. Imagine your money story as this living, breathing thing that changes every time you make a choice about money. It's influenced by every feeling you have about spending, saving, or even just talking about money.

Reflect on the moment when money truly held significance for you. It could have been receiving birthday money and feeling like the wealthiest kid in the neighborhood, or it could have been realizing how financially difficult things were at home. How you first learned about money, whether through saving or spending, shapes your financial habits today, which may not align with your family's.

Reflect on how your family's approach to money impacts how you feel about it today. Was money the ticket to happiness in your house, or was it more of a source of stress? How your family dealt with money, how open they were about financial struggles or successes, and how they responded to your wants and needs all feed into your own story about money.

Making connections between your past and your current perspective on money can be enlightening. Whether you've picked up a sense of generosity, caution, or something else from your upbringing, these early influences are the seeds of your personal money narrative.

I remember when James worked with me, we had to unpack his childhood memories as we worked through his money stories. His feeling of not feeling deserving stemmed from a time when he was riding in the back of his dad's car afterschool, and he asked, "Can we get McDonald's?" The dad turned back and looked at the nine-year-old boy and sternly asked, "Do you have money for that?!" Being able to identify those moments enabled James to work through building worthiness and confidence again and feeling that he could ask for help when he needed it.

To truly understand your money story, reflect on your past, identify significant moments and emotions related to money, and comprehend how those experiences shape your current perception of money. This step can bring up all sorts of feelings, but tackling it with a bit of kindness towards yourself helps you make sense of your financial journey. Realizing that your past money moves were based on what you knew and felt back then is key to reshaping your money story to fit where you want to go next.

(And no... I did not get in trouble for popping the balloon.)

Chapter Takeaways:

- Your money mindset is a powerful driver behind how you handle finances, influencing not just your actions but also your emotional response to money.

- Early experiences and the beliefs about money you absorb from those around you play a crucial role in forming your money mindset, often without you realizing it.

- Limiting beliefs about money, such as feeling unworthy or fearing success, can prevent you from achieving financial prosperity and need to be identified and challenged.

- Reflecting on your personal money story, including your earliest memories of money and how your family dealt with finances, can provide insights into your financial behaviors and beliefs, offering a path to rewrite your financial future.

Action Step:

Reflect on your earliest memory involving money. Write down how it made you feel and consider how it might have shaped your current beliefs about money.

BONUS MATERIAL

The **"REWRITING YOUR MONEY STORY WORKBOOK"** is your essential guide to financial empowerment. Uncover and understand the money stories that shape your financial behavior, and transform them into a positive, empowering narrative. Achieve lasting financial abundance and confidence through reflective exercises, thought-provoking prompts, and practical activities.

JUST SCAN THE QR CODE RIGHT HERE OR VISIT THE LINK BELOW TO ACCESS YOUR **FREE BONUS!**

SCAN ME

www.jenmoneycoach.com/the-creative-code-book-bonuses

6 Changing Your Money Reality and Beliefs

"Financial liberation starts with a seed of change in your mind. Plant it, nurture it with positive beliefs, and watch your reality transform into a garden of abundance."

JEN FONTANILLA

As I walked into the sales manager's office, memories flooded back of the time I nervously presented my collection of projects that I had worked on as a print broker. Just out of college, I was trying to find something better than the little mom and pop print shop for which I had been making simple business cards and flyers. The company was well known in the corrugated industry for making displays and packaging for the movie industry, a specialized sector of the print world that I had practically no experience in, other than the one display I did for a local tea company. But I knew, no matter what, I would figure it out because I always do.

He looked across the big wooden desk at me and asked, "How much do you want?" I loved that question! It would be the first time I felt the incredible power of being able to say what I wanted, not being told what they were going to pay me. With confidence as strong as steel, and a whole lot of "I have no idea what I'm doing" going on in my head, I replied, "$40 an hour, and if I have to stay past eight hours in a day, it goes up to $55."

"Done."

No objections. I felt this surge of energy run up my back as I thought in my head, "What?! It was that easy?! Just ask?" It was then that I realized the power of believing in what you're worth and having fearlessness in asking for it. Granted, I delivered above and beyond and knew that I could because I knew my skillset. From that moment on, aligning money to what I knew I deserved and what I was worth became a fun game to play. Moreover, I found that I thoroughly enjoy the art of negotiation without becoming emotionally invested in the outcome. Whenever I faced rejection or unmet requests, I simply said, "It's not going to work out," and reassured myself, "It wasn't meant to be." There is something else waiting for me.

If you can master changing your beliefs about who you are and what you deserve, God will continue to present opportunities for you, like gifts waiting for you to open them.

So, as we begin this chapter on changing our stories and beliefs, I encourage you to ask yourself these things: Who do you want to be, what do you want to do, and what do you want to have? Be, do, and have. Believe that you are deserving of it all.

As my mentor, Kisma, always says (and a line that I borrowed for my TEDx talk), "We are who we believe ourselves to be." So, who do you believe you are? If you don't like the answer, here we go. We're about to change that.

Transforming Your Money Story

The power to change your money story lies entirely in your hands. It starts with a willingness to confront and challenge your existing beliefs. Are they serving you well, or are they hindering your financial well-being? This introspection can lead to profound revelations and the motivation to adopt new, more empowering beliefs.

Your money story is not just about where you've been; it's also about where you're going. With intention, reflection, and action, you can shift from a narrative of limitation to one of abundance and fulfillment. In this chapter, we're going to go deeper into changing your money story and, more importantly, your beliefs.

Remember, you hold the pen, and you have the power to rewrite your story in a way that aligns with your values, dreams, and goals. Here's to the beginning of a beautiful new chapter in your financial journey. Don't forget to enjoy the journey just as much as the destination.

T. Harv Eker suggests that to really get a handle on your money matters, you need to kick those negative money beliefs to the curb and adopt some positive ones. This shift in thinking is like resetting your financial thermostat, so you start feeling more at ease with making and managing more money.

Before you can start embracing positive money vibes, you've got to tackle those negative thoughts about cash that are dragging you down. Without understanding the reasons behind your money mindset, those deep-seated beliefs will persist and prevent you from transforming your financial behaviors. This was a common roadblock I noticed as a financial advisor—people struggling to follow their financial plan, splurging too much, or too scared to invest, all because they hadn't dealt with the underlying issues fueling their money fears. It's like that buddy who always says, "I just can't save! I end up in debt no matter what."

Let's take an example. Imagine you're trying to build up the positive belief that you can invest your money smartly. But, if deep down you believe that money is the root of all evil, you might end up feeling guilty just for wanting more of it. This hidden belief can trip you up, leading to delays in investing or not-so-great investment choices, often without you even knowing why you're doing it.

Let's identify and ditch those negative money beliefs, swap them for some empowering thoughts, and start feeling like we've got a firm grip on our finances.

Here's how we'll break it down in four steps:
1. Ignite the drive to tackle your money beliefs.
2. Spot the negative beliefs you hold about money.
3. Examine and reshape those negative beliefs.
4. Match your actions to your shiny, new positive beliefs.

1. Ignite the drive to tackle your money beliefs.
Feeling stuck and unable to shift your money thoughts can really throw a wrench in your plans to overhaul those limiting beliefs.

To get that motivational engine running, start by laying out what it's costing you to stick with your current money mindset. Ask yourself, "What am I losing out on, both financially and emotionally, by not changing my mindset?"

Basically, what opportunities are slipping through your fingers?

Then, balance those costs against the advantages you could enjoy by shifting to a more positive and empowering view of money.

You can pinpoint these advantages by considering three key questions:

- What positive changes will you notice in how you feel about yourself after making this shift?
- In what ways will this transformation boost your overall happiness?
- How will this change positively affect the people you care about?

Here's another exercise to help you clarify these consequences and benefits.

Write down everything you desire and everything you'd rather avoid when it comes to money.

For instance, you might say: "I don't want to spend my whole life working. I don't want to always be an employee. Instead, I want to enjoy leisure and fun times with my children without the stress of needing to make more money. I want to shop for groceries without any guilt."

2. Spot the negative beliefs you hold about money.

Nailing the first step will clarify the perks you're aiming for by shifting your money mindset. Next up, let's figure out the specific beliefs that are getting in the way of your financial control and the enjoyment of these perks.

Chances are, you're not fully aware of your deep-seated beliefs about money, so spotting these limiting beliefs will take a bit of detective work. Experts recommend looking at how you think, feel, and speak about money as clues. You'll know you've hit on a disempowering belief if it sparks doubt about your capabilities or if it stirs up negative feelings that make you feel trapped.

Whenever you catch yourself in a negative thought loop, take a moment to consider what underlying beliefs might be fueling those thoughts. For instance, if you find yourself thinking, "I'll never be able to afford anything nice," it might be rooted in a deeper belief like, "No matter how hard I work, I'll always be just scraping by."

Listening to how you talk about money can reveal a lot about your limiting beliefs. Check out these phrases; they're big clues to those kinds of thoughts:

- Pointing fingers for financial woes: "It's the economy's fault I'm not earning what I want."
- Envying others' success: "They act like they're better than everyone else."
- Justifying not having much money: "It's fine; money isn't everything."

- Griping about your money situation: "My job is terrible, and the pay is too low."

- Restricting your own options: "I can't chase wealth and still be there for my loved ones."

- Doubting your worth: "I don't deserve to make more money."

- Obsessing over setbacks and fears: "I won't try because I might mess up."

- Setting sights low for comfort's sake: "Why bother working harder than necessary?"

3. Examine and reshape those negative beliefs.

After pinpointing those limiting beliefs, it's time to dive deep into understanding them. You'll want to think about where they come from, their effect on your financial life, and what good might come from releasing them.

By shining a light on these beliefs, you can see clearly how they're affecting your money matters and start moving towards more positive, empowering thoughts.

To get to the heart of each limiting belief, consider asking yourself these five questions:

- **What sparked this belief in the first place?**

  Take, for instance, the belief that your financial woes are someone else's fault, which could stem from hearing your parents blame economic conditions for their money issues.

- **How does this belief shape my view of myself, others, and my experiences?**

  Building on the example above, thinking it's always someone else's fault could lead you to feel powerless about your financial situation and possibly resentful of those who seem to have it easier.

- **What changes might occur if I embraced the opposite belief?**

  Imagine you start believing you're in full control of your financial destiny. You might view every financial obstacle as an opportunity to grow and boost your confidence in managing your money.

- **How would I think differently if my beliefs were aligned with financial success?**

  You could begin to see any financial mishaps as learning experiences on your path to better money management rather than reasons to place blame.

- **What positive beliefs could I adopt moving forward?**

  Opt for a belief like, "I own my financial situation, and I'm open to learning from my setbacks."

4. Match your actions to your shiny, new positive beliefs.

Once you've worked through those five questions, you'll end up with a set of beliefs geared towards boosting your financial control. Now, let's talk about how to truly embrace these beliefs.

Start aligning your actions with the empowering beliefs you've chosen. Kick things off with a small but meaningful step that reflects one of your new beliefs. For instance, if you're aiming to see yourself as a saver, go ahead and put a bit of your paycheck into a savings account that earns interest.

This initial action starts a positive cycle, reinforcing your new, constructive beliefs. Changing your behavior for the better leads to outcomes that feel rewarding. So, when you see that first deposit grow, even just a little, it boosts your sense of achievement and strengthens your belief in your financial management skills.

These positive outcomes fuel your commitment to sticking with your new habits and inspire you to make even more constructive changes, keeping that good feeling going strong. Watching your deposit grow with interest serves as a motivator to keep adding to your savings and gives you the confidence to explore other smart money moves, like investing in stocks or other ventures.

Once you've taken action in line with your empowering beliefs, turn those actions into habits. For instance, make it a routine to stash away any leftover cash at the end of each month or check on your account's interest progress every week. The more you repeat these new behaviors, the more you reshape your brain, weakening the grip of old, limiting beliefs that once held you back.

In his book "Atomic Habits," James Clear explains how aligning your habits with your chosen beliefs drives effective belief adoption by tying actions to identity. As you consistently act in accordance with these beliefs, your sense of self starts to shift accordingly. So, if you consistently behave as though you already hold empowering beliefs, you'll naturally start to embody those beliefs, reinforcing the cycle.

For instance, dedicating an hour each week to financial review can gradually mold you into someone who's financially responsible. This newfound identity will drive you to keep up with financial tracking and wise money management because that's simply what financially responsible individuals do.

Conquer the hurdles of behavior change, recognizing that it might stir up some mental pushback. It's common to feel fear or come up with excuses to avoid making changes; this resistance naturally arises when challenging long-held beliefs and routines.

To overcome this mental resistance, start by pinpointing your negative thoughts and allowing yourself to acknowledge and release any accompanying emotions. Then, visualize the positive outcomes you anticipate from altering your behaviors. Additionally, pose uplifting and empowering questions that guide you toward fulfilling solutions.

For instance, if you're hesitant about setting up a budget, ask yourself, "How can I make budgeting effortless and even enjoyable?"

A Few More Things to Solidify Your New Beliefs

Reflect and Rewrite

Your emotions and imagination are powerful tools in reinforcing these beliefs. If your old narrative was about the struggle to make money, shift that picture to one where abundance flows easily to you.

Visualize it, immerse yourself in the feelings it brings, and start taking small, daily actions that align with this new belief. Buying yourself something nice as a reminder that you deserve good things can be a simple but powerful affirmation.

Affirm and Act

Incorporate these new beliefs into your daily affirmations. Say them out loud, write them on post-it notes around your house, or set them as reminders on your phone. But here's the crucial part – let these affirmations guide your actions. Beliefs turn into reality through consistent, aligned action. If you believe you're worthy of financial abundance, what steps do you need to take to align with that belief? Maybe it's investing in your skills, asking for that raise, or setting up a savings plan.

Magnetizing Your Desires

Your new beliefs aren't just passive statements; they're actively drawing experiences and opportunities toward you. Believing in your ability to make a living doing what you love, for instance, opens up a world where your passions and financial abundance go hand in hand. This shift in belief transforms how you attract, spend, and relate to money.

Remember, if there's something you desire but don't yet have, it might be a belief holding you back. By identifying this belief, you're paving the way for new opportunities and experiences that resonate with your true worth and potential.

Cultivating a New Self-Image

As you adopt new beliefs, your self-image begins to evolve. This transformation is not just about feeling worthy of more money but extends to every aspect of your life. From inviting more joy and connections to dressing in ways that reflect your newfound confidence, these changes are all reflections of the inner belief that you deserve abundance.

Celebrate Every Step

Remember, every step towards your new belief system, no matter how small, is a victory. Celebrate it! Whether it's catching yourself before you fall into an old thought pattern or taking a small step toward your financial goals, each action is a testament to your commitment to your new story.

The Vibrational Match

And let's not forget about the universal and spiritual laws you've been exploring. By shifting your beliefs and aligning your actions, you're also working on matching the vibrational frequency of abundance. The Universe loves a good co-creator, and by stepping into your power and embodying your new beliefs, you're sending out a pretty powerful RSVP to prosperity.

The Power in the Words "I Am"

In the world of positive vibes and spiritual journeys, saying "I am" is kind of like sending a text message to the universe. Think of it as your personal way of telling the world who you are and what you're all about. But here's the kicker: the words "I am," if you choose to follow them, are super important. It's like choosing the right emoji—it sets the whole tone! When we say something like "I am strong" or "I am happy," it's not just a feel-good statement; it's like planting little seeds for our future. Imagine that every "I am" is a magic spell. What comes after those words can bring amazing things into your life or hold you back if you're not careful. So, it's really important to pick words that make you feel abundant, love, or whatever it is you desire. Words that lift you up, words that sparkle, and words that make you believe you can do anything. Because in the end, the "I am" magic is all about creating a beautiful story for yourself, one where you're the star. So, we should also be mindful of when we say negative or harmful words about ourselves after "I am."

When working with Oma, she had such a deep desire to pursue copywriting. She was so sick and tired of her job, but she learned to stay grateful because it was paying the bills. But she wanted more than anything to focus on copywriting. She would doubt if she had the ability to pursue this and if her work was worth the price she asked for. Oma would ask herself questions such as, "Is it really true that no one would hire me to do this work?" Then, she recalled the people she met at a networking event who were excited for her to work on their email newsletter campaigns. She started regularly finding actual instances that would generate doubt in what she had been telling herself. She began to say, "I am prosperous. I am marketable. I am attracting the right clients to work with me." Soon after, her belief in herself and her work continued to grow, and she now looks forward to promoting and marketing her writing skills to coaches and creators.

Crafting new beliefs to transform your money story is a journey of empowerment, creativity, and alignment. It's about breaking free from the scripts that no longer serve you and stepping into a role that feels authentically yours. So, keep leaning into this process, stay curious, and remember – you're not just rewriting your money story; you're transforming your life.

What new beliefs are you excited to bring into your life today?

● ● ●

Chapter Takeaways:

- Take charge of your financial narrative by challenging existing beliefs and embracing empowering ones.

- Shift from a narrative of limitation to one of abundance through intention, reflection, and action.

- Address negative money beliefs to prevent them from hindering your financial progress.

- Adopt empowering beliefs through introspection, reflection, and aligned action.

Action Step:

Write down a new, empowering money belief on a small piece of paper each morning, such as "I attract financial abundance effortlessly." Carry this note in your wallet or pocket throughout the day as a physical reminder of your commitment to transforming your relationship with money.

7 Unlocking Abundance with Daily Affirmations

*"Affirmations serve as bridges between the person you are
and the limitless being you are destined to become."*

JEN FONTANILLA

How many times have you written a positive statement on a Post-it note and stuck it on your bathroom mirror or the side of your computer monitor? Most of us have done it at some point. Affirmations are our personal cheerleaders that scream phrases like "I have unlimited abundance" that you tell yourself to bring out the magic in your everyday life. It's all about the here and now, speaking truths into existence by believing in the power of your thoughts to shape your reality.

Affirmations are more than just feel-good quotes; they're a secret weapon for mindset magic. When you're pouring everything into your work, affirmations are like a bridge linking your creative fire to your beliefs about your own value and the abundance you can attract. They remind you that you're not just valuable for what you create but for who you are, helping you see the wealth in your worth.

When you sprinkle these affirmations into your daily routine, you're basically opening up your heart and mind to the endless possibilities that life has to offer. It's like aligning yourself with God's, the universe's, your Higher Power's grand plan, tapping into your soul's deepest desires, and

• • •

inviting all kinds of goodness to come your way. Imagine it: more abundance, more joy, and more of what makes your heart sing.

Now, it's super important to pick affirmations that flow with you. If the words don't fit quite right, switch them up. The whole point is for these affirmations to feel good and in alignment with who you are. They should resonate with your very being, making them all the more powerful. And hey, why not craft your own? Get creative and pen some prosperity affirmations that are uniquely you.

Most affirmations kick off with "I."

This "I" is huge—it's not just about your everyday self; it's about the whole package: your higher self, your soul, that inner part of you that's all kinds of connected to the divine spark within. When all these parts of you are in harmony, singing the same tune, affirmations become this incredible force for change.

Feel free to play around with the wording. If "I am the source of my abundance" doesn't quite hit the mark, maybe "My soul is the source of my abundance" feels more on point. The idea is to find phrases that light a spark in you.

For affirmations to work their magic, they've got to feel doable. Saying you've got a million bucks in the bank right this second might be stretching it if you're not quite there yet. Start with something a bit more believable, like boosting your income by 10%, and build from there. Success breeds success, after all.

So, how can you activate the power of affirmations in your life?

- **Repetition:** Dive into the book, pick out affirmations that call out to you, and then settle in to repeat them over and over. There's immense power in repetition, rewiring your subconscious to accept these new beliefs and kickstart changes that mirror this newfound inner truth.

- **Sync with your breath:** Try linking each affirmation with your breath. Inhale, lifting the affirmation to your higher self, and exhale, releasing it into the world to work its wonders.

- **Visual reminders:** Jot down those affirmations and pepper them around your space—anywhere you'll catch a glimpse regularly, especially the ones that really strike a chord. This constant visual cue reinforces your journey towards manifesting your desires.

- **Choose resonant statements:** Select or create affirmations that genuinely resonate with you and your goals. They should feel meaningful and possible, even if they challenge you slightly.

- **Consistency is key:** Make affirming a daily habit. Whether first thing in the morning, during a break, or before bed, find a routine that allows you to focus and repeat your affirmations regularly.

- **Embody the feelings:** As you recite your affirmations, try to embody the feelings and emotions they evoke. Visualize achieving what you're affirming and embrace the emotions associated with that success.

- **Incorporate them into various activities:** Affirmations can be integrated into meditation, journaling, or even creative practices. This variety can help reinforce their messages throughout your day.

- **Speak them aloud:** There's so much power in voicing your affirmations. Speaking them aloud reinforces their impact, making them more believable to yourself.

Be Mindful...

When leveraging affirmations, keep these streamlined guidelines in mind to maximize their impact:

- **Stay grounded:** Choose realistic affirmations that stretch your ambitions without straying too far from reality.

- **Action and affirmation:** Pair affirmations with concrete actions towards your goals for a synergistic effect.

- **Feel your words:** Tap into your emotions. If an affirmation feels off, it might indicate a need to adjust your approach or mindset.

- **Make it personal:** Customize affirmations to fit your unique goals and circumstances for greater resonance.

- **Be patient and persistent:** Understand that change is a process. Consistent, repeated affirmation use over time gradually reshapes your mindset.

- **Believe:** Reciting words without belief is futile. Your affirmations should be phrases you can truly stand behind.

- **Routine matters:** Incorporate affirmations into your daily life to subtly shift your subconscious over time.

- **Face negatives:** Don't gloss over negative emotions; confront and understand them to ensure affirmations aren't just a cover-up.

- **Present and positive:** Phrase affirmations in the present tense to emphasize immediate relevance and positive change.

Let's reflect on the essence of integrating affirmations into your creative journey. Tailor your affirmations to mirror your unique artistic visions and goals. Let them be the guiding light that aligns with your personal aspirations and the broader horizons of your career. Use these affirmations as your shield against the inevitable creative blocks and fears, turning them into stepping stones that propel you toward greater creativity and flow.

Visualize your success with each affirmation. This practice doesn't just amplify the impact of your words; it leverages your inherent imaginative prowess, making your affirmations a potent force for change. In moments of doubt or setback, let affirmations be your reservoir of resilience, reminding you of your unwavering strength, adaptability, and the intrinsic value of your creative endeavors, independent of external accolades.

Create an environment that breathes your affirmations. Whether through inspirational notes, art, or digital cues, let your surroundings be a constant echo of your inner voice of affirmation. And remember, affirmations gain deeper roots when intertwined with practices like meditation, journaling, or your unique creative rituals, anchoring them firmly in your daily life and work process.

Besides reading and writing affirmations, I also verbally speak them out loud every day. I have adopted a phrase that I learned from my mentor, "I am infinite energy, I am prosperity, I am love." I will repeat that for a few minutes. Have you ever had the intention to start a habit but never follow through? I use habit stacking to remember to do this each day. Every morning after I leave my kickboxing class, I say that phrase on repeat as I drive home. Now, I don't ever forget, and I say it every day.

● ● ●

Tread this path with patience and kindness towards yourself. Change unfolds in its own time. Celebrate every step forward, however small, and treat yourself with the compassion you deserve. Your journey with affirmations is one of experimentation and evolution; as you grow and evolve, so too should your affirmations. Let them evolve to reflect your changing landscape, ensuring they remain a powerful catalyst for creativity, growth, and fulfillment.

In embracing affirmations, you're not just adopting a practice but cultivating a mindset that transforms obstacles into opportunities, doubts into confidence, and dreams into reality. Let this chapter be a reminder that within you lies an unbounded potential waiting to be unleashed through the power of affirmations.

Chapter Takeaways:

- Affirmations should be realistic and resonate with your current situation and future aspirations.
- Emotions evoked by affirmations are important; they should be explored, not ignored, for deeper insight.
- Affirmations are not a standalone solution; they should be accompanied by actionable steps and magnificent action toward your goals.

Action Step:

Start today by selecting one affirmation that resonates deeply with your creative spirit and aspirations. Write it down on a piece of paper and place it where you'll see it every day. Make it your mantra for the week, and each

• • •

time you see it, take a moment to repeat it aloud with conviction and visualize its truth manifesting in your life and work.

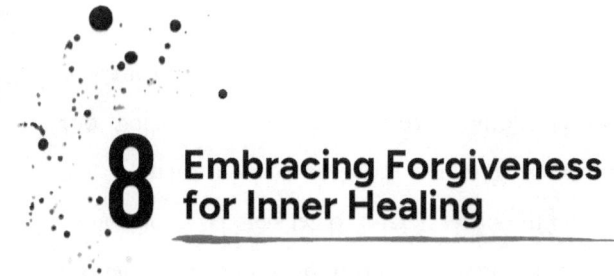

8 Embracing Forgiveness for Inner Healing

"Forgiveness isn't a transaction; it's a transformation—a sacred alchemy where pain becomes liberation, and wounds become wellsprings of creativity and abundance."

JEN FONTANILLA

Money, at its core, isn't just paper and coins; it's energy, a frequency that dances to the beat of our inner vibrations. When we align ourselves with the energy of abundance, generosity, and love, we open doors to creative and financial prosperity we never knew existed.

But here's the catch: to tune into this frequency, we need to lighten our load. Imagine carrying a backpack filled with 100-pound rocks—each rock representing resentment, bitterness, or unhealed wounds. These burdens skew our frequency, pulling us away from the abundance we're capable of attracting.

Creating space and forgiveness are deeply intertwined concepts that go hand in hand, especially when we consider our emotional and spiritual well-being. At its heart, forgiveness is about releasing ourselves from the grip of past hurts, grievances, or disappointments. It's a process of letting go that clears away the emotional clutter blocking our path to growth, happiness, and abundance.

Forgiveness is the process of removing those heavy rocks from our backpacks. It isn't about condoning wrongdoings or dismissing our feelings. It's about acknowledging that holding onto resentment is like drinking poison and expecting the other person to get sick. By choosing to forgive, we're not doing a favor for those who wronged us; we're setting ourselves free. Free to create, to love, and to attract prosperity.

Forgiveness tunes our vibrational frequency to one of liberation and creativity. It's a powerful tool not just for healing relationships with others but, more importantly, with ourselves. So, how do we embark on this journey of forgiveness and self-love?

The Weight of Holding On

When we hold onto grudges or bitterness, it's like cluttering our internal landscape with heavy stones. Each stone represents a story, a wound, or a piece of unresolved business that weighs us down, making it hard to move forward freely. This weight can stifle our creativity, dampen our spirits, and block the flow of positive energy and opportunities into our lives.

Forgiveness, in its essence, is an act of clearing away these stones, one by one. It doesn't mean forgetting what happened or condoning it; rather, it's about releasing the emotional charge it holds over us. This act of letting go creates space within our hearts and minds—a spaciousness that allows new experiences, ideas, and energies to enter.

The Ripple Effect on Creativity and Abundance

This clearing has a particularly transformative impact on creative professionals. Creativity thrives in open, unencumbered spaces. When our emotional landscape is cluttered with unresolved feelings, our creative flow is disrupted. We might find ourselves stuck, unable to express ourselves freely or to connect with our true vision and voice.

Furthermore, forgiveness opens the door to abundance. By letting go of past hurts, we align ourselves more closely with the vibrational frequency of abundance. We signal to the universe that we are ready to move beyond our past limitations and welcome new opportunities for growth, prosperity, and success.

Forgiving Those Who Hurt Us or Don't Believe in Our Dreams

There are going to be people in our lives, oftentimes it's our own parents, family, or friends, who will not understand what we're doing or that these dreams of ours are passions deep within us that need to be fulfilled. This is where forgiveness for these people is going to be crucial because it's not our job to convince others or be, what my mentor has taught me, in the right. How often do we want to prove and fight? But where does it get us? Bitterness, hurt, and anger, and as you know from Chapter 2, are low vibrational frequencies, and I'm sure we're not trying to attract more of that.

So, when it comes to people who don't understand your dreams, the best thing you can do is to lean on your value, who you are, and remember that you don't have to take on their money stories or beliefs. The power of choice allows you to rewrite your own story, even if it contradicts those who don't support your endeavors. This is about living out your passion, deciding what you want, choosing what will be the highest and best frequency for you. You might have to be bold and challenge the status quo.

● ● ●

If you don't, I guarantee you that there will be disappointment. The question will be whether the disappointment will be on the other people's end because you didn't follow what they told you to do or within yourself because you chose not to fulfill your dream. The choice is always your superpower.

Letting Go of Our Own Past Mistakes

Sometimes we need to forgive ourselves in order to let go of the past to make a move towards a brighter future. You know, every choice you've made so far? Yeah, they all added something to your life. Certain decisions led to personal development, while others completely transformed your life, but ultimately, they were the right choices given the circumstances. And sure, you might scratch your head now, wondering, "Why the heck did I do that?" but believe it or not, each choice, even the questionable ones, helped shape you into who you are today.

Forgive yourself when you look back into the past and think of things like, "I made some pretty stupid decisions with the things that I bought. I should have bought that property years ago, and now I would have lots of money. I shouldn't have made that investment that totally bombed! I shouldn't have lent that money to that friend; I knew I would never get it back!" Those kinds of thoughts can hold you back from greater abundance. Drop your pictures of times in the past when situations did not work out as well as you wanted. When negative thoughts come up, disregard them and reflect on moments when you made wise financial decisions, felt satisfied with your purchases, achieved a good return on an investment, or were repaid by a friend. As you forgive and love your past self, focusing on all the times you have succeeded, you change the course of your future.

Practical Steps Towards Forgiveness

Embarking on the journey of forgiveness can present obstacles, yet by implementing practical strategies, we can navigate this path with greater ease.

1) **Acknowledge the hurt:** Recognize the feelings and emotions associated with the situation. Allow yourself to feel them without judgment.

2) **Decide to forgive:** Make a conscious decision to forgive, not for the other person, but for your peace and freedom.

3) **Release the emotions:** Use techniques like journaling, meditation, or even talking to a trusted friend or therapist to process and release the emotions.

4) **Visualize the release:** Imagine sending off the hurt and pain, perhaps as leaves floating down a river, signifying the emotional clutter being cleared away.

5) **Embrace the space:** Notice the new space within you. Fill it with positive affirmations, creativity, and openness to abundance.

Remember, your creative and financial abundance begins with the relationship you have with yourself. By practicing forgiveness and self-love, you clear the path for your creative energy to flow freely, attracting prosperity and joy into your life. So, take a deep breath, let go of those burdens, and step into the vibrant, creative life you deserve.

Transformative Practices for Practicing Forgiveness

To heal and unlock our fullest potential, forgiveness is an essential step that encompasses self-love, creativity, and financial growth. Beyond the exercise previously discussed, there are other powerful practices to facilitate this process. Here's a closer look at three transformative methods: the Ho'oponopono Prayer, the Mirror Exercise, and Writing and Burning Letters. Each practice offers a unique path to releasing old wounds and embracing a life of abundance and peace.

HO'OPONOPONO PRAYER

Ho'oponopono is an ancient Hawaiian practice of reconciliation and forgiveness. It involves repeating four simple yet profound phrases:

"I'm sorry."

"Please forgive me."

"Thank you."

"I love you."

This prayer, like a mantra, can be directed towards oneself, others, or even inanimate objects and situations, recognizing the interconnectedness of all and how our own healing can impact the world.

How it works: By repeating these phrases, we acknowledge our responsibility in the creation of our life experiences, ask for forgiveness for our part in any pain or suffering, express gratitude for the lessons learned, and affirm love for ourselves and others. This process helps to clear negative energies and restore harmony within and with others.

How it Helps: The Ho'oponopono Prayer helps in releasing resentment, guilt, and anger, facilitating a deep inner healing process. It brings about a state of peace and acceptance, allowing for the flow of positive energy and creativity. It teaches us the power of love and forgiveness, and its repetitive nature helps to reprogram the subconscious mind towards positivity and self-love.

THE MIRROR EXERCISE

The Mirror Exercise involves standing in front of a mirror, looking into your own eyes, and expressing forgiveness and love towards yourself.
This can be challenging at first, as it requires confronting your own vulnerabilities and insecurities head-on.

Here's how to do it: Position yourself in front of a mirror, make eye contact with yourself, and initiate a conversation as if you were talking to a beloved friend. You can start by apologizing for the ways you've been harsh or critical towards yourself, followed by expressing understanding, forgiveness, and unconditional love. You may also use this exercise to forgive others by visualizing them in the mirror and directing your words of forgiveness towards their image.

How it Helps: This exercise helps break down the barriers of self-judgment and criticism, fostering a compassionate and loving relationship with oneself. It can also aid in releasing resentment towards others, as seeing them through your own reflection helps humanize them and understand their actions from a place of empathy and compassion. This practice strengthens self-esteem and facilitates a deeper emotional release, making space for healing and creativity.

WRITING AND BURNING LETTERS

This practice involves writing a letter to yourself or someone else, expressing all the unspoken feelings, grievances, and emotions you've been holding onto. The act of burning the letter serves as a symbolic release of those emotions, transmuting the energy from thoughts to paper and finally to smoke, allowing it to dissipate into the universe.

How to Do it (Safely): Write your letter in a private and calm setting, pouring out all your feelings without holding back. Once you're done, find a safe place to burn the letter, such as a metal sink, an outdoor fire pit, or a large, fire-proof bowl. Light the letter on fire, and as it burns, visualize the negative emotions and energies being released and transformed into peace and forgiveness.

The Significance: This ritual is powerful in its ability to transform energy. It allows for a tangible release of pent-up emotions, facilitating closure and healing. By physically letting go of the letter, you symbolically release the hold that past hurts and resentments have on you, paving the way for higher vibrational energies like love, peace, and creativity.

How it Helps: Writing and burning letters can be incredibly cathartic, helping to release anger, shame, and other low-frequency emotions that block our ability to forgive and move forward. It clears the mental and emotional space needed for healing, self-love, and creative expression, aligning us with our true potential and the abundance of the universe.

Each of these practices offers a unique pathway to forgiveness, self-love, and, ultimately, a life filled with creative abundance and financial prosperity.

• • •

By incorporating them into your daily or weekly rituals, you can start to heal the wounds of the past, embrace the present with open arms, and step confidently into the future you deserve.

As we journey through this exploration of forgiveness and its profound impact on our lives, a lingering question may arise: "What does this have to do with my money?" The answer lies in understanding the vibrational essence of our universe, where everything, including money, operates at specific frequencies. Forgiveness, a powerful act of letting go, not only heals our hearts but also clears the energetic space around us, allowing us to align with the frequencies of abundance and prosperity.

What's this got to do with money?

At first glance, the connection between forgiveness and financial success may seem obscure. Yet, at its core, money is a form of energy that flows to and from us, much like the tides of the ocean. Holding onto grudges, harboring resentment, or wallowing in guilt and shame keeps us stuck in lower vibrational frequencies. These negative emotions act as barriers, repelling the positive energy flow and, by extension, the financial abundance we seek.

When we choose to embrace forgiveness through practices such as Ho'oponopono, the Mirror Exercise, or writing and burning letters, we create a powerful energy transformation. This shift is not just emotional or psychological; it's vibrational. Forgiving ourselves and others lifts the heavy burdens of anger, guilt, and shame, replacing them with love, peace, and gratitude—emotions that resonate with the frequency of abundance.

Forgiveness opens our hearts and expands our capacity to receive. When we clear the clutter of negative emotions, we make space for blessings, creativity, and, yes, financial prosperity. It's akin to tidying a room; only when we remove the unnecessary clutter can we appreciate the beauty of the space and welcome new treasures into it.

Moreover, having forgiveness promotes a mentality of abundance. It encourages us to let go of victimhood and scarcity thinking, empowering us to take control of our lives and our finances. It shifts our focus from what we lack to the abundance we can create and attract. This positive mindset is magnetic to opportunities, ideas, and the right people who can lead us to financial success.

I have this funny phrase now that goes like this: *Breakups lead to breakthroughs.* One day, I opted to write a letter where I acknowledged the important individuals in my life who have caused me pain. I began each letter with "Dear..." followed by their name, expressing my emotions, and explaining why I felt hurt. I then ended it with a thought around "thank you for teaching me or showing me...." It was essential that I held onto gratitude for the lessons, the good things, and every other thing, whether good or bad, is part of our journey. I know that forgiveness is for my healing and to let go. I can find peace in knowing this is a part of my growth. I then took the letters and walked outside to the backyard and burned them. I watched the paper disintegrate into the air. I transmuted energy and set it free. I didn't have to talk to these people, I didn't have to explain anything. I just released and remained in gratitude and felt this release and space free up within me.

Our personal growth and spiritual evolution are essential aspects of the journey towards financial abundance. Forgiveness is a key component of this journey, facilitating a deeper connection between us and the universe. It transforms our relationship with money from one of stress and struggle to one of joy and ease.

So, as we close this chapter, let's step forward with open hearts, ready to receive the abundance that awaits us.

Chapter Takeaways:

- Forgiveness is essential for emotional and spiritual well-being, freeing us from past hurts and opening doors to growth and abundance.

- Letting go of grudges clears space for creativity and opportunities, allowing positive energy to flow into our lives.

- Practical steps like acknowledging hurt, deciding to forgive, and releasing emotions are key in the forgiveness process.

Action Step:

Allocate a peaceful moment for introspection and compose a letter of forgiveness. This letter may not be intended for sending. Start by addressing it to the person or situation you wish to forgive. Express all your feelings, the hurt, the disappointment, and the impact it has had on you. Then, shift towards forgiveness, writing statements like, "I choose to release this burden from my heart," or "I forgive you and let go for my peace." Conclude by envisioning the emotional space this act of forgiveness is creating within you, allowing for new energy, creativity, and abundance.

After completion, you have the option to retain, discard, or symbolically let go of the letter (for example, by tearing it up or safely burning it). This physical act of writing and releasing symbolizes the emotional process of forgiveness and the creation of new space within your life.

9 Purging to Create Space for Creativity and Wealth

"When you release what no longer serves you, you're creating a vacuum that the Universe eagerly fills with blessings and abundance."

JEN FONTANILLA

If you're anything like me, your desk over the course of a week fills up with pieces of paper with notes on them, Post-its of different colors scattered on the edges of the second monitor, and pieces of to-do lists here and there. I eventually get to a point where I can feel myself hit a capacity limit and I have to just stop. "I cannot stand this freaking mess anymore." Because before I even attempt another day of trying to just push through again, I can't help but feel the mess staring back at me. And so, I begin to throw away, organize, make my neat little piles of "to keep" or "to throw" or "later." But even after a few minutes (and if you've done this yourself you know where I'm going with this) you finally sit down, take a deep breath and exhale, "NOW I'm ready to work!"

Our creative flow and financial well-being are greatly influenced by clutter in our physical and energetic environment.

At its core, making space is about removing barriers to allow energy to move freely. Money, in its essence, is a form of energy and a great one. When we clear out what no longer serves us—be it physical clutter, outdated beliefs, or lingering resentments, or certain relationships or friendships —we're essentially creating a clear path for new opportunities and abundance to find us.

Clearing away obstacles in your conscious and subconscious minds, as well as your physical environment, is crucial for thriving in prosperity.

Clutter: The Creative Block

Ever noticed how that cluttered workspace can leave you feeling uninspired or even anxious? That's because clutter is a physical manifestation of stuck energy. It not only disrupts the flow of creativity but also mirrors the chaos within, making it harder to attract the abundance we seek. By decluttering our spaces, we're not just tidying up; we're setting the stage for money, ideas, and positive energy to flow into our lives. You must clear the way and make space for whatever you want to come into your life.

We're all beings of energy—every element in the vast Universe resonates with it.

Clearing away obstacles in your conscious and subconscious minds, as well as your physical environment, is crucial for thriving in prosperity.

The Physical Clutter

Imagine your home or workspace as a river, and clutter as a dam blocking its flow. Just like that, physical clutter creates a bottleneck for the energy of abundance. When our surroundings are chaotic and overflowing with stuff we no longer need, it's like putting up a "Do Not Enter" sign for prosperity. By decluttering, we create room for abundance to flow into our lives.

A cluttered space can act as a magnet for stagnant energy and a breeding ground for negativity. Think about it: when your surroundings are in disarray, it's like rolling out the welcome mat for chaos and disorganization to make yourself at home. Pay attention to how you feel when you enter or leave your living space, office, or any area you spend time in. If you notice a significant shift in your mood or energy levels, it's a pretty clear indicator that unwanted vibes have set up camp.

Creating a harmonious environment begins with a purge of the physical reminders of negativity. This includes anything from old photographs that dredge up unhappy memories, to books, clothes, and even pieces of furniture that no longer serve you or bring joy. Essentially, if it evokes feelings of sadness or unease, it's time for it to go.

Once you've decluttered, you can use one of the many energy-clearing rituals available to scrub away the residual negativity from your space.

The final touch is to infuse your space with positivity. Think about what elements you can introduce or alter to invite happier, healthier energy into your home, as these changes can transform your physical environment into a welcoming sanctuary of positive vibes.

So, what can we do to make space?

Get rid of unnecessary items. Removing unnecessary items can create a more open and inviting atmosphere in your home, allowing in more natural light. If you're unsure about what to keep or let go, consider what you truly love and use regularly versus what rarely gets attention. Sometimes, just reorganizing or storing items away can refresh your space and your mindset. It's about finding a balance that works for you and your home's energy.

Let in fresh air. One of the simplest methods to dispel negative vibes in your home is to freshen it up. Open your windows wide, get the fans going to keep the air moving, and even open up those closets and drawers to shake off any stagnant energy hiding in there. Consider stepping out for a bit while your home breathes, and maybe light some incense or sage when you come back.

Burn incense. Incense works wonders for banishing negative energies. Light up a stick or cone, and let it work its magic, driving away any unwelcome vibes and cleansing your space. Palo santo, a fragrant wood from South America, is especially good for this. It's said to be a powerful purifier. Simply ignite one end, extinguish the flame, and allow the smoke to weave through your room, carrying away negativity.

Do a smudging ceremony. The sage smudging ceremony is an effective method to eliminate any negative vibes hanging in your space. By lighting a dried sage bundle, you can purify your room or entire home. White Sage is known for its cleansing properties, driving away negativity when burned correctly. Allow the sage to burn for about 10-20 seconds before extinguishing it. Next, place it on a fire-resistant surface like an abalone shell.

Place houseplants around. Taking care of indoor plants creates a calm and tranquil atmosphere. Historically, houseplants have played a role in maintaining the health and happiness of homes, and caring for them boosts a sense of well-being. Moreover, they help purify the air, adding energy and vibrancy to your living space.

Set up a personal sanctuary. Setting up a home altar can be a straightforward but impactful method to infuse your space with positivity and mindfulness. Choose items for your altar that symbolize prosperity, luck, health, abundance, or safety, keeping in mind that everything placed there should reflect what you wish to attract into your life. Consider including candles, crystals, incense, figurines, photographs, books, flowers, and any other elements that resonate with your aspirations.

Light candles. Healing and spiritual practices have long been associated with candles. Lighting candles can deepen your meditation or enhance other spiritual rituals. Placing them around your home not only boosts the ambiance but also infuses your space with positive energy. It's important to choose high-quality candles, as many budget-friendly options made from paraffin wax and synthetic fragrances may release harmful chemicals.

Place crystals. People all over the world use healing crystals to cleanse and protect their bodies, homes, and workplaces. The best way to use them is as the last step in a cleansing ritual. Feel free to position a crystal in any area of your home where you aim to dispel negative vibes or draw in positive energy. Protective stones like Obsidian, Amethyst, Black Tourmaline, Tiger's Eye, and Citrine are excellent choices for warding off undesirable energies and cleansing the atmosphere of negativity.

Discard Worn-Out Clothes and Accessories. This is a big one, even for me. If we say that we want to embrace luxury or opulence or want "nice things" and wealth to come into our lives, how can we expect that to happen if we're holding on to clothes or accessories or things that are just falling apart? If they are still usable, consider donating them to a cause or organization. However, it's time to show that we are ready for more quality in all aspects of our lives.

The Clutter in Our Mind

Physical clutter is a little easier to identify, but we also need to get rid of our mental clutter. So, who or what needs a gentle goodbye to make room for this flow? It might be old projects that never took off, relationships that drain rather than inspire, or even self-doubt that clouds our worthiness, it can even be saying goodbye to those clients who are draining (you know the ones where you cringe when you see them on your caller ID. Yes, those ones.) Identifying these blocks is the first step toward clearing them.

Get rid of "one day" thinking. We often keep a lot of things because we believe we might need them in the future. My cousin and I laugh about this because our parents are notorious for keeping everything because of the "just in case" mentality. But what ends up happening is we end up with old National Geographic magazines from 1985 and the old Betamax tape rewinder all stored in the garage. Let. It. Go.

Time to say goodbye. Saying goodbye is necessary. I've had to silently part ways with relationships and friendships weighed down by stuck energy. I was conscious that it was what prevented me from moving forward, caused financial setbacks, and occupied my thoughts. Despite the pain and sadness, I understood its importance for my well-being. I made the decision to forgive and move on, creating space in my heart, spirit, and body for release and letting go. Sometimes these were friends, romantic partners, even clients or colleagues.

One simple thing I would ask myself is "Does this relationship drain me or fill me, and does it align with who I am and my values?" Many times, I would just sit in silence during meditation, and I would observe how my body felt when asking myself that question. It was honest and revealing and, in those moments, I knew when I had to release and let go. But it was so healthy, and I knew that I needed that. I needed it so that I could fully show up for myself, my son, the people who valued me and my clients.

Sometimes it's some family members. I have had to coach some clients that have had difficult times with their own parents, and they had to learn how to what I call "love from afar." It doesn't mean you cut people out of your life (unless you're obviously in physical or mental danger or harm) but it's establishing those boundaries so you can breathe and function and honor what you need.

Jot the idea down. According to Mark Hurst, the brilliant mind behind the NYT bestseller *Bit Literacy,* juggling endless to-dos in your head or constantly being bombarded by emails and texts disrupts your brain's ability to tap into its creative flow. It's like trying to run multiple programs on a computer with limited RAM—it slows everything down. This mental clutter not only impairs your ability to filter information but also weakens your working memory.

The solution? Give your brain a break! Choose a handy online tool, app, or good old-fashioned pad of paper to offload your tasks. By dumping everything into one organized space, you clear the mental clutter and give your brain the room it needs to focus and thrive.

I know whenever I meditate and pray, that is when I get the most ideas flowing into mind! I know it's because I'm relaxed and allowing my brain to think. So, I always have a notepad or paper and a ton of pens next to me because I have to write. Think about how many times you didn't write that idea down and even seconds later you're asking yourself, "Dang it! What was that thing I just thought of?!" Write it down.

This is what's crazy: Consuming an excess of digital information can clutter your brain just like physical clutter overwhelms your space. So, we need to be mindful of how much we're consuming.

Journaling or morning pages. I want to encourage you to get the clutter off your mind by doing morning pages, a concept I was introduced to from the book *The Artist's Way* by Julia Cameron which is a form of journaling. You can write down things you're worried about, plans on how to achieve an important goal or anything that's causing you stress. You can't do it wrong. The book talks about helping you unblock yourself and get in touch with your creative side.

This practice entails writing three pages of longhand, stream-of-consciousness writing as the first activity of your day. Here are the guidelines for morning pages:

- Commit to writing daily
- Use pen and paper

- Begin immediately after you wake up
- Fill three pages
- Write freely, allowing whatever thoughts you have come to mind without interruption

Writing morning pages offers numerous benefits, including increased clarity and focus, enhanced creativity, emotional release, improved problem-solving skills, self-discovery, heightened productivity, and stress reduction. By engaging in stream-of-consciousness writing each morning, you can declutter your mind, uncover insights, and set a positive tone for the day ahead, promoting mental and emotional well-being. It's a discipline for sure!

Creating space isn't just about decluttering; it's a transformative process that impacts every facet of our lives. It invites us to evaluate what we truly value, shedding what no longer fits. This not only rejuvenates our creative spirit but also reinforces our self-worth and readiness to welcome abundance in all forms.

By embracing these practices, you're not just tidying up; you're setting a powerful intention. You're affirming your worthiness of success, creativity, and financial freedom. And in this space of openness and clarity, you'll find your creativity knows no bounds, and your capacity to attract wealth and opportunities is limitless.

When I talked earlier about clearing my desk, I also created that space to welcome the things that make my workspace one that I like to be in. You can choose which things you want to implement. I moved my desk so that I could see the snow-capped mountains from a distance during the winter, feel the sunshine, I have a succulent plant on the right-side corner of my desk (his name is Shrek), I have a little crystal tree by my monitor and a candle that burns while I write. Enhancing the energy of your work environment can have a significant impact on your mood and productivity. So, try some of these simple ways to incorporate this into your workspace.

When you declutter your life—letting go of things you no longer use or need, and shedding relationships that no longer serve you—you create space for the Universe to work its magic. It's like making room for new guests at a crowded party; once you clear the way, something you truly desire is likely to step in and fill that void. Prosperity will not flow into a mind or a home that is full of clutter. The very act of clearing will create a vacuum that the Universe will fill.

Chapter Takeaways:

- Clutter hinders creativity and prosperity: Just as clutter on a canvas stifles an artist's creativity, physical and energetic clutter obstructs our creative flow and financial well-being.

- Making space invites abundance: Clearing physical, mental, and emotional clutter creates pathways for energy to move freely, inviting opportunities and abundance into our lives.

- Clearing mental and physical clutter: Decluttering not only our physical spaces but also our minds and relationships is essential for thriving in prosperity.

Action Step:

Take 10 minutes today to declutter one small area of your home or workspace. Start with a drawer, a shelf, or a corner that feels overwhelming. As you clear away the physical clutter, notice how it creates a sense of spaciousness and calm. Notice how this small act of decluttering shifts your energy and opens up room for abundance to flow into your life.

BONUS MATERIAL

These "**JOURNAL PROMPTS**" provide a space for reflection and release. Through ten insightful prompts, you'll identify and clear out mental and emotional clutter that may be hindering your financial and creative abundance. By purging these limiting beliefs and patterns, you'll create the energetic space needed to manifest your highest potential and welcome prosperity into your life.

JUST SCAN THE
QR CODE RIGHT
HERE OR VISIT
THE LINK BELOW
TO ACCESS YOUR
FREE BONUS!

SCAN ME

www.jenmoneycoach.com/the-creative-code-book-bonuses

10 Renewing Your Spirit by Clearing Your Energy

"In the art of energy clearing, we become architects of our own inner space, sweeping away doubts and fears to make room for the sunshine of possibility."

JEN FONTANILLA

We all have those days where we feel like a sponge in a sea of vibes, soaking up a little too much of everything around us. It's like walking through life with sticky fingers, collecting bits and pieces of everyone else's emotions, thoughts, and, yes, even their drama. Suddenly, you're carrying around a backpack full of energies that aren't even yours, wondering why you feel heavier, like it's Thanksgiving Day dinner.

I have this friend—let's call them Alex. Alex is the kind of person you can't help but love to bits, the kind you'd be there for if they ever needed anything. But, every time we caught up, I felt this overwhelming sense of heaviness, like a blanket of fog rolling in, clouding my mood and my energy. At first, I brushed it off, thinking maybe I was just tired or having one of those days. But then, it hit me—I was absorbing all of Alex's negative energy, from the never-ending cycle of complaints to the problems that seemed to follow them around like a shadow. Whenever we spent time together, it felt like being caught in a dust storm, leaving me dirty and longing for a shower, both physically and emotionally.

You see, just like me trying to shake off that dust, we all have moments where we need to clear away the energy that clings to us. Whether it's the aftermath of a not-so-great meeting or combative client, the emotional toll of scrolling through social media making you question if what you're doing is good enough, or just the daily dance of dodging negativity, we need to be proactive about keeping our energy clean and vibrant. Because, believe it or not, our energetic hygiene is just as crucial as our physical hygiene.

But imagine feeling lighter, more focused, and so at peace that you wonder how you ever carried around all that excess energy. Clearing out energy that doesn't align with your best life can make you feel amazing.

From simple boundary-setting exercises to practices that help you tune into your own vibes, we'll explore ways to make room for more of what you want in your life and less of what you don't.

Negative energy is like that uninvited guest who crashes your party and then refuses to leave, affecting your mood, your health, and even your sleep.

Clearing energy helps our creative output by allowing us to embrace the present moment and feel a sense of worthiness and abundance. When we clear our energy, we become grounded, centered, and focused. We release our emotions, purify our mental space, and make space to attract that we desire. As we enhance our self-worth and emotional state, we invite wealth and opportunities into our lives, establishing a positive bond with our money.

I'll share a few of my favorite ways I clear my energy, the ones I sneak into those precious break times (thank you, Pomodoro method.) From the small, everyday adjustments to the deeper, transformative practices, we're going to shake off that dust and step into a brighter, lighter version of ourselves.

Protecting Your Energy

While we can clear our energy, it's also important to know how to protect it in the first place. Let's look at some simple ways to do this.

First, tune into how you're feeling. Sometimes, we're going so fast that we haven't stopped to breathe and even think and feel what we're feeling. Identify that first. It's astonishing that they are oblivious to how their busyness makes them susceptible to external energies, absorbing ones they should reject. I want to say, "Stop! Please breathe!" It's crazy how they don't realize that they are so busy being busy that they're so easily influenced by the energies around them and that they are absorbing the kind of energy they need to repel.

Set boundaries to conserve energy. We need to have discernment when we are giving our energy away. Are you saying "yes" to everything? If so, do you end up feeling like you don't even have anything left in your tank for yourself? This is where it's important to practice boundaries. When we do this, we don't feel run down, and we're able to stay in higher vibration throughout our day. When we are mindful of our decisions in terms of what we're saying yes to, we also limit our exposure to energy-depleting people and activities.

Be aware of your triggers. Does excessive stress lead to anxiety? Absolutely. Protect your energy by recognizing and handling stress triggers. If deadlines cause you to retreat in discomfort, master the art of organization. Feel uneasy in social settings? Opt for gatherings that genuinely excite you rather than attending out of obligation. Remember, politely saying "no, thank you" or "I'll pass" shows remarkable strength.

Triggers are a huge one for me. One thing that I learned is to stop and pause when there is a trigger that I experience from a situation or someone else's words and I ask, "What else could this mean? This is a trigger, what is going on here? Why am I taking this personally?" I will often find that the trigger is connected to something in the past and usually does not have to do with the person right in front of me. I use this as a teaching and growing moment. It also helps me to conserve my energy and not fall into a lower vibration of anger, jealousy, or shame.

Build a bubble of light or a metaphorical wall around you. To protect yourself from negative energy, creating a barrier is an extremely effective method. Similar to envisioning your happy place, this method leverages the strength of visualization. Inhale deeply, close your eyes, and imagine enveloping yourself in a gentle, white, positive light. Picture it as a protective bubble, a force field, or akin to beneficial light therapy. Regardless of the term you prefer, it serves as a robust means to fend off negative energies.

Get a grip on your ego. Consider how much vitality you squander in response to negative forces, expending it on matters of little significance. Take a moment to sincerely reflect on how obsessed you are with having a perfect social media image, or how easily you get caught up in arguments fueled by gossip. Your ego is in full swing whenever you react to detrimental vibes, fret about matching someone's appearance, or endeavor to alter someone's perception of you. Before responding, take a moment to pause. Refrain from allowing your ego to dictate your actions or deplete your energy. Consider if the situation is deserving of your valuable energy.

Protecting your energy is crucial for your overall well-being, as it directly influences your happiness. Daily, we pour much of ourselves into our jobs, friendships, and relationships. It's essential to acknowledge that our needs hold equal importance as those of others. Safeguard your energy. Give yourself the gift of a truly healthy mindset.

Clearing Your Energy

I have a variety of methods for clearing my energy, but I'll focus on the ones I use most often.

Visualization: Seeing it in my mind's eye

Think of it as daydreaming with a purpose. You're already a pro at imagining vivid worlds and stories in your work, right? Now, imagine applying that superpower to your life goals, including your financial ambitions. This is where we get to picture ourselves achieving our desires, the ideal outcomes, and what it is we want to be, do, and have.

Visualization is like sketching your aspirations into the universe's suggestion box. It involves visualizing a vivid image that motivates your brain to turn it into reality. When it comes to money, picturing yourself as financially successful and secure can help overcome subconscious barriers and limiting beliefs that may hinder your progress.

Meditation: Getting centered

Far from just a tool for relaxation, meditation can be your secret weapon against the chaos of the creative process. It helps you clear out the mental clutter, quiet the self-doubt, and tune into your inner wisdom. Think of it as maintenance for your brain, creating the space and clarity needed for ideas to flow freely.

For the money mindset, meditation can be transformative. It allows you to observe and shift those sneaky thoughts and feelings about money that might not be serving you. Regular practice can help you cultivate a sense of peace and abundance, which, believe it or not, attracts more of the same into your life.

Nature Walks

I make it a point to go for a walk every day and immerse myself in nature - observing the blooming flowers and plants, nocturnal animals venturing out in daylight, and people walking their dogs. This is also a time for me to get away from devices and the computer and just appreciate God's creation and admire the beauty that's around us. It allows me to be grateful and appreciative.

Grounding

Grounding, also known as earthing, is a therapeutic method that involves activities that reconnect you to the earth. This method is based on the concept that physical contact with the earth can provide health benefits by transferring free electrons into the body. It feels powerful just standing in any of these and feeling connected and reenergized.

Breathwork

Explore different breathwork techniques to help regulate your energy. Techniques such as 4-7-8, box breathing, or pranayama can help calm the mind, reduce stress, and clear energy blockages. Again, because we are so used to being busy, we sometimes forget to just breathe. Slowing down our breath allows us to get oxygen flowing through our bodies and again is a way to just clear out chaotic energy within us.

Cord Cutting

This has got to be my favorite one. Cord cutting is a powerful, energetic practice that's aimed at releasing and healing emotional ties that no longer serve your highest good. It's based on the idea that we form energetic "cords" with people, places, situations, and even past experiences, which can continue to affect our energy and emotional state long after the interaction has ended. These cords can drain our energy, keep us stuck in the past, or create ongoing emotional discomfort or imbalance.

The main purpose of cord cutting is to reclaim your energy and establish healthy emotional boundaries. This tool is powerful for letting go of past relationships, healing from traumas, or breaking free from any energetically binding situation. By severing these cords, you're essentially allowing yourself to release the emotional and energetic baggage that may be hindering your personal growth, peace of mind, and even your creative and financial prosperity.

How to Practice Cord Cutting

- **Set a Clear Intention:** Begin by setting a clear intention to release the connection that no longer serves you. It's important to approach this practice from a place of love and forgiveness, both for yourself and the other entity involved, rather than from anger or resentment.

- **Visualization Meditation:** Find a quiet space where you can meditate without interruptions. Close your eyes and visualize the cord that connects you to the person, situation, or experience you wish to release. Imagine this cord extending from your energy field to the other entity.

- **Cutting the Cord:** In your visualization, see yourself holding a pair of scissors, a sword, or even just your hand as a blade—whatever resonates with you—and gently but firmly cut the cord. As you do this, affirm to yourself that you are releasing the connection with love and gratitude for any lessons or experiences it provided. I'll even say, "Cut the cords" as I create a sweeping motion in front of me, behind me, to the sides of me. Then I imagine I am gathering them together in a bundle, putting them into a container in the ground, and putting a lid on top of it. I repeat this maybe 3 to 5 times.

- **Healing the Space:** After cutting the cord, visualize a healing light or energy sealing the area where the cord was attached to you. This helps to heal the space and ensure that your energy remains intact and protected.

- **Closure and Cleansing:** Conclude the practice by grounding yourself. To physically cleanse your energy, try taking deep breaths, grounding yourself, or even taking a shower. Reflect on the sense of freedom and lightness that comes with releasing these ties.

- You can do this a few times throughout your day, after a phone call or conversation, or anytime you feel congested energy taking over.

One of my favorite things to teach clients is how to visualize. Every day when I do this, I see in my mind the things that I journaled about, the desires within my heart, the people I want to help, the stages I want to talk on, the group gatherings I want to be a part of, the fun trips and adventures I want to experience, the dream home workspace I would love to design, the ideal partnerships I want to be involved with. As I close my eyes, I imagine and feel everything as if I'm already there, making it feel real. When we bring in the emotions, we anchor this within our mind. Be as detailed as you can. Imagine reaching your goal or desires: How does it feel? What are your surroundings? How does reaching that goal impact you? Impact those around you? Who is with you? Getting emotional with your mental imagination is another important part of the overall practice.

After you've tried a method of clearing your energy, it's important to reflect on how you feel - before and after. Try to ask yourself questions such as "How do I feel after the cleansing?" or "What part of this process did I like the best?" By doing this, you'll be able to see if there are certain aspects of the process that you prefer to remove unwanted energy.

Chapter Takeaways:

- Recognize when you're absorbing too much from others, and it's weighing you down, kind of like carrying a backpack full of rocks that aren't yours.

- Set boundaries to prevent ending up emotionally drained; it's deciding who and what deserves your energy, and who doesn't make the cut.

- Keep an eye on your ego to make sure you're not wasting energy on stuff that doesn't really matter in the grand scheme of things, like social media drama or pointless arguments.

- Engaging in energy-clearing practices regularly, like visualization, meditation, nature walks, grounding, breathwork, and cord cutting, not only helps shake off negative vibes but also boosts creativity, self-worth, and openness to abundance and opportunities.

Action Step:

Schedule a "digital detox" period into your day, even if it's just for 30 minutes. Use this time to disconnect from all electronic devices and engage in an activity that nourishes your soul, like reading a book or taking a nature walk.

11 Improving Your Relationship with Money and Magnetizing Wealth

"Money speaks the language of attention and respect; talk to it with your actions and watch your financial situation flourish."

JEN FONTANILLA

Imagine you have a friend you haven't seen in quite a while. She's been making efforts to reconnect, reaching out with calls, texts, and even sending cards. Despite her efforts, you keep making excuses or struggling to find time to meet her. You keep dodging her, not because she's a bad person or that you've had a falling out - you just keep on being too busy. What do you think is eventually going to happen? Yeah, she's going to feel like you don't value her as a friend and might just eventually stop trying to even hang out or come by.

Now imagine if that friend was money.

Have you ever thought of money as a friend? Your approach to money can greatly influence its flow in your life, even if it's an unconventional idea. Negativity, like saying, "I can't stand you" or "I wish I didn't have these bills," sends out vibes to the universe that you don't value money. In turn, money might just decide you're not someone it wants to stick around. Changing your dialogue to welcome money and showing it respect and care can make a world of difference by attracting more of it into your life.

This section isn't just about saving more or spending less; it's about reshaping how you interact with money on a fundamental level. You'll see money not as a source of stress but as a friend that supports your journey towards self-worth, creativity, and abundance.

Napoleon Hill once pointed out the power of our thoughts, suggesting they magnetize our brains to attract the forces, people, and circumstances aligned with them. This magic, attributed to a higher power or the universe, underscores the immense potential within us to create our reality through our mindset and energy.

Our thoughts don't just linger in our minds; they shape our attitudes, actions, beliefs, and the energy we emit. Consequently, it is vital to sustain a positive and lucid thought process. Clarity about what you want attracts more of it, reducing the chances of undesired outcomes. It's about embracing your power to choose and pursue your deepest dreams.

Explore various approaches to cultivate a welcoming and appreciative attitude towards money, allowing it to flow abundantly into your life.

Embrace Abundance

The law of abundance is evident everywhere, especially in nature. By appreciating and surrounding yourself with abundance and prosperity—whether in the places you dine, the quality of your purchases, or the company you keep—you elevate your own energy field toward wealth. Spend more time with those who embody an abundance mindset, doubling down on positivity over negativity. An author working in a beautifully designed, light-filled studio embodies this principle, leveraging their environment to inspire unlimited creative potential.

Permission to Prosper: From Guilt to Generating Wealth

Guilt about prosperity can sabotage your financial magnetism. A common myth is that wealth is finite, implying your gain is someone else's loss. This scarcity mindset can hinder your success in sales, business, and beyond, dampening your wealth-attracting energy. Remember, there's an infinite abundance out there. Letting go of guilt and embracing an abundance mindset strengthens your attraction power. For creative professionals it is so crucial to understand that charging what you are worth, like a graphic designer setting rates that reflect their creativity and skill, doesn't take away from anyone else.

Discover Methods for Generating Additional Income

Here's a fun challenge: List 50 ways you could make more money. This isn't about limiting expenses but opening up to the possibility of generating more wealth. It could be anything from creating posts for someone's social media to selling handmade jewelry. This exercise can help shift your focus from scarcity to abundance.

Live Authentically Rich

Acting "as if" doesn't mean living beyond your means for show. It's about authentic expressions of wealth in your lifestyle choices, attire, and environment. This authenticity in living a prosperous life, even in small ways, aligns your energy with the abundance you seek. I remember there was a time when all I could do was walk through a high-end furniture store and just imagine it being in my home or maybe ordering a cocktail at a beautiful bar in Downtown LA just to enjoy the scene.

We may have our seasons where it's just not happening and we're just trying to get by but be creative. Find little ways to allow opulence into your life and just surround yourself with it, even if for a moment and savor all the feels that come into your heart and being at that moment and welcome it.

Have Faith in Your Financial Journey

Embrace the ebbs and flows in your relationship with money, keeping faith in the long-term vision for prosperity and happiness.

Embarking on this journey of transforming your relationship with money into a loving and supportive partnership opens up new pathways to abundance and joy. Each step, infused with intention and care, paves the way for a more fulfilling and prosperous life. Remember, the quality of your relationship with money mirrors the love and attention you're willing to invest in it.

Know Your Numbers

Clarity about your finances, including goals and current standing, is essential. Let go of past financial missteps and focus on gratitude and opulence. Familiarize yourself with your numbers to pave a clear path toward your financial dreams. For example, a freelance web developer setting and tracking income targets showcases the importance of financial clarity for creative professionals.

What gets measured gets managed. Keep track of your income, expenses, and savings. This doesn't have to be complicated—a simple spreadsheet can do wonders. Seeing your financial picture clearly can inspire more informed and confident decisions.

Giving Your Money the Attention, Priority, and Openness It Deserves

Giving your money full, undivided attention is the secret sauce to making it grow. It's all about presence and mindfulness, acknowledging every dollar and cent as part of your journey to abundance.

Now, imagine setting up a date night, but instead of with a person, it's with your finances. Yep, you heard that right—create "Money Dates" even if it's by yourself (of course, you could do it with your partner or spouse to make sure you're on the same track.) Mark it on your calendar just as you would a romantic dinner or a catch-up with a friend. During these sessions, dive into your budgets, investments, savings, the whole shebang. It's your time to connect, understand, and appreciate your financial situation, fostering a deeper, more intimate bond with your money.

I remember the days when I would visit a client, and I would see a big envelope or binder full of unopened envelopes of their investment statements or their insurance policy stashed in their kitchen drawer. Fear and disorganization kept them from giving their money and investments the attention it needed. This can be a prosperity block if we are treating our money this way.

Elevating money's priority in your life doesn't mean obsessing over it 24/7. It's about aligning your actions with your values. When you show money the respect and attention it deserves, it starts to play a more significant, positive role in your life. It's like watering a plant; nurture it with the right attention and watch it thrive.

And one more thing - talking about money shouldn't be taboo. Growing up we've likely heard that money discussions are a no-go or something best kept under wraps. But why should it be? Wealthy folks have been onto something for ages—they talk about money openly, sharing tips, mistakes, and lessons with family and friends. It's high time we break the silence. Start small, talk about daily expenses, savings goals, or even your latest budgeting app find. The more you talk, the more demystified and manageable your finances will become. And this is even more critical if you have kids. Remember the chapter about money stories? What kind of money stories are you creating for your own children? Are you modeling an abundance mindset and openness towards your finances for them or are they seeing that this is something secretive and scary?

By integrating these practices into your life—giving money your full attention, prioritizing the place your financials occupy in your life, and opening up about financial matters—you're not just managing money, you're building a relationship with it. And like any good relationship, it's built on attention, respect, openness, and, yes, a bit of love. Start giving our finances some love and witness the abundance they bring in return.

Shifting Financial Perspectives: From Excuses to Empowerment

Transitioning from a mindset of blame to one of empowerment and innovation is just the beginning. When we perceive challenges as chances to grow and innovate, just like a musician making a distinct sound with limited resources, we tap into a new realm of financial creativity and resilience.

It's also crucial to cultivate a spirit of self-compassion along this journey. Just as you would easily forgive a friend for a mistake, it's essential to extend that same understanding and grace to yourself when it comes to financial missteps. Learning from these experiences and moving forward without self-reproach sets the stage for a healthier relationship with money. Often, our emotional reactions to money—whether frustration, stress, or dissatisfaction—are not about the numbers themselves but reflect deeper, underlying beliefs and attitudes. By examining and realigning these beliefs, we can significantly improve not only our mood but our financial well-being, too.

Moreover, embracing financial curiosity can transform the way we view our monetary landscape. When faced with unexpected financial situations, adopting an attitude of curiosity rather than judgment encourages a deeper understanding of our finances. This proactive approach not only demystifies complex scenarios but also equips us with the knowledge to make informed decisions, ensuring we're better prepared for future financial endeavors.

Speaking Wealth into Existence

There is power in your words. The way you talk about money reflects your underlying beliefs and energy towards it. Speak of wealth, love, health, and spirituality with positivity and gratitude to align your actions and attract abundance. Start your day with positive affirmations about money. Say them out loud, write them on Post-its, and repeat them to yourself. This practice can help shift your mindset from negative to positive, empowering you in your financial journey.

Conscious Spending: Balancing Gratitude, Needs and Wants

Whenever you find yourself at the checkout line or clicking the "buy now" button online, pause for a moment and infuse that action with a hearty dose of gratitude. Repeat to yourself, "There is an endless supply of opportunities." At the same time, cultivating a keen awareness of the fine line between wants and needs becomes pivotal. This wisdom enables you to navigate your financial decisions with greater clarity, ensuring that each expenditure not only brings you joy but also aligns with your essential life requirements. Adopting this approach fosters a more balanced and fulfilling financial life, where gratitude opens the doors to abundance, and discernment ensures your resources are directed toward what truly matters.

Giving Creates Blessings

Giving or tithing from a place of joy expands your capacity for wealth, creating a cycle of giving and receiving rooted in universal abundance. A video producer donating part of their project profits to support young filmmakers demonstrates how creative professionals can prioritize savings and giving, reinforcing the cycle of abundance. You could also find a nonprofit to give your time to and teach classes, be a mentor, or support their fundraising efforts because it aligns with your creative values.

Write a Love Letter to Money

Yes, you heard me right. Grab a pen and paper and pour your heart out to money. Despite its unconventional approach, this method effectively helps you express your feelings and intentions about money. Express gratitude, outline your hopes, and invite money into your life as a partner in achieving your dreams. Here's an example:

> *Dear Money, I know I haven't been around much, and I keep ignoring you. I don't look at my statements or app alerts about what's going on with my accounts; I don't know my exact balances - I know I've been neglectful, and I'm sorry. I want to do better. I'm going to spend time with you each week and create a plan of what I need to do to get things under control. I also want to say I'm grateful that you're in my life because you do provide the things I need and the resources to enjoy and have fun once in a while.*

It's a way for you to get real and in touch with what's going on and to show appreciation for money being in your life.

Making Your Wallet a Home

How's your wallet looking these days? Crumpled bills, worn-out leather, old receipts, and cards strewn about? Think of your wallet as money's home. By keeping it tidy and respecting the physical form of money, you're sending a clear message to the universe: "I value and take care of my money." It's a simple step with powerful symbolic significance. It just might be time for you to go shopping and do some house cleaning with your wallet.

Here's an interesting one I have been doing for years - carry a $100 bill into your wallet or purse to keep a slice of abundance with you. Try not to spend it. It's there to remind you that there's a whole lot more where that came from. Think of this money as a little nudge from the universe, showing you what's possible. Remember the affirmations? When you say, "I always have money." This is definitely true. You do truly have money. Just because you don't have all the cash you want right now doesn't mean it won't ever show up. Imagine there's an endless supply of money out there, and yours is just waiting to find its way to you.

Take Meaningful Action

Wealth gravitates toward those with wealth consciousness, who understand the importance of serving humanity while maintaining a detached stance toward money. Action is a testament to your readiness to receive; it signals to the universe that you're in sync with your desires and willing to meet them halfway. A photographer launching a personal project on environmental conservation demonstrates how creative professionals can align their craft with their values through meaningful action.

I remember the first time I saw my mentor speak at a conference several years ago, she had us do this interesting exercise. "Get your wallets out," she lightly commanded. Back then, I struggled to comprehend much about this and how to cultivate a mindful connection with our finances. But I remember feeling a sigh of relief that I had been gifted a beautiful Coach wallet for my birthday the year before. But my goodness, before that, I was using a terrible zippered pouch, which I think was originally meant for makeup. I was mortified to think that that was what housed my money. No wonder I was broke! Since then, I have talked about that exercise, and I always look forward to what the next home upgrade for my money will be.

Embrace these principles as part of your journey towards wealth. Remember, the key to attracting wealth lies in the synergy of your thoughts, words, actions, and the energy you bring to every moment. It's about prosperity in every sense—money, love, success—however you define a rich life.

Chapter Takeaways:

- View money as a friend: embrace money with positivity and respect to invite more of it into your life.
- Surround yourself with abundance: live and act in ways that reflect abundance, enhancing your wealth attraction.
- Let go of guilt: embrace your worth and the abundance you deserve, without feeling guilty for aspiring to wealth.
- Live authentically and richly: infuse your lifestyle with small, authentic expressions of wealth to align with abundance.

Action Step:

Open your wallet and tidy it up, ensuring it's a respectful and organized home for your money, then place a $100 bill (or the highest denomination you're comfortable with) inside to symbolize and remind you of the abundance you're welcoming into your life.

12 Recognizing Your Worth and Elevating Your Self-Value

*"Embracing your worth is the first step to unlocking a life
where abundance flows as freely as your belief in your infinite potential."*

JEN FONTANILLA

It's time to talk cash and how to get cozy with it because, let's face it, you deserve to be paid what you're worth. When you undervalue your time and energy, you're basically throwing a big old roadblock in your path to abundance. Money vibes with your energy. It likes to flow where it's respected and welcomed. So, crank up the value you place on your skills, and watch how that cash begins to flow your way, smooth and sweet, rewarding you for standing up for your worth and honoring both yourself and others.

Now, I get it. A lot of folks out there are scratching their heads over why they're not getting the pay they expect. They're crossing their fingers, hoping someone will notice their worth and throw extra bucks their way. Spoiler alert: Hoping someone else will value your worth without you declaring it loud and clear is like waiting for a bus at a train station. When you rock a solid sense of what your services are worth, trust me, others will start to pick up on that vibe, too. Take the reins and set your own price tag—figure out what your time really means to you, what kind of paycheck or contract spells success in your heart. Don't sit around waiting for someone else to put a value on your worth. Make it your mission to peg your own price tag. Figure out what your time really means to you, what sort of return feels juicy, and go get it. Remember, if a deal feels good to you and them, it's a win-win. Everyone's happy.

Now, here's a trap I see all the time: "I'll just slash my rates to pull in more clients." Hold up a minute. If you constantly trim your fees below what feels right, you're not just giving yourself a raw deal; you're also clogging up your money flow. Trimming your rates can breed resentment and whispers to your subconscious that your work isn't worthy. It's like putting up a 'Closed' sign on your own opportunity shop. Instead, start treating yourself with a little more love. Command the fee you genuinely believe you're worth.

Know your value, honor your worth. One of the biggest high-fives you can give yourself is recognizing that you're making a real difference. You're not just making money; you're helping folks build their dreams. That's the real jackpot.

This isn't about changing who you are; it's about embracing and enhancing what you've always been. Imagine stepping into a version of yourself that not only sees your own worth but lives by it every single day. That's where we're heading, and trust me, this journey will not only alter how you perceive yourself but revolutionize your relationship with money. Why? Because how you value yourself directly influences the abundance you allow into your life.

Everything in the universe, including money, operates at a specific frequency. When you value yourself, you emit a frequency of abundance, becoming a vibrational match for wealth and opportunities. It's like tuning into a radio station where the music of prosperity plays endlessly. By aligning your self-worth with the energy of abundance, you naturally attract financial opportunities and wealth into your life.

This investment is not unnoticed by the universe. Like attracts like, and as you pour energy into your advancement, the universe mirrors this by presenting opportunities that match your elevated state of being. Opportunities for wealth creation begin to flow more freely towards you, not because you're desperately seeking them, but because your increased self-worth and confidence signal to the world that you're ready and capable of handling more.

Self-worth acts as a magnet for abundance in all forms. When you believe in your value, you make decisions from a place of abundance rather than scarcity. This mindset shift opens you up to take calculated risks, explore new opportunities, and embrace challenges as pathways to growth and wealth. The universe responds to this boldness by manifesting opportunities that align with your expansive view of yourself.

Here's how you can start living in harmony with the wealth you're meant to attract:

1. **The Ultimate Declaration: Claim Your Respect**
   Right off the bat, make a promise to yourself: No more begging for love, respect, and attention. The kind you ought to be showering on

yourself? Start now. If you're not treating yourself like royalty, who will? Embrace the fact that there's nobody quite like you. Celebrate your individuality and let go of the need to measure yourself to others.

2. The Comparison Trap: Why You Feel Undervalued

The heart of the matter? Comparison. It's a sneaky thief of joy, making us believe we're never enough, not smart enough, not successful enough, not *anything* enough. It's a depressing cycle that only drags us down. Let's put an end to that, shall we?

3. Know Your Worth: The Foundation of Self-Respect

Not recognizing your worth leads to a domino effect of settling for less—less than desirable jobs, unworthy partners, and undervaluing your own potential. It's time to know and embrace your worth. Only then can you stop selling yourself short and start demanding the amazing life you deserve.

4. Beyond Knowing: Increasing Your Value

Understanding your worth is one thing; increasing your value is another. Always room for improvement, folks! Don't get cocky and think you're the bee's knees with no room to grow. Flaws? We all have them, but they shouldn't define us or ruin our chances at happiness and healthy relationships.

5. House Hunting Analogy: Unleash Your Full Potential

Imagine you're a house with a potential value of $500K, but right now, you're sitting at $300K because of neglected repairs. Don't expect to attract buyers (or in life, opportunities, and relationships) at your full value without doing the necessary work to showcase your true worth. Similarly, we must invest in ourselves, addressing our flaws and enhancing our strengths to fully realize our value. It's about presenting the best version of ourselves to the world, not hiding behind our imperfections.

6. **Staging Your Best Self: Embracing and Improving**

    You've got to stage your life like that house. Show off the best version of yourself, not the fixer-upper version. Work on those issues because being open to constructive criticism is crucial. It's not about taking every comment to heart but discerning which feedback can propel us toward our potential. This openness to improvement reflects a deep self-respect and an understanding that growth is a lifelong process. Compare yourself only to who you were yesterday and celebrate your progress. Set goals, seek out new experiences, and always strive to be the best version of yourself.

7. **Core Genius: Identifying and Amplifying Your Strengths**

    What are you freakishly good at? What makes you, you? Recognize your strengths and build on them. Remember, it's your opinion of yourself that truly matters. Don't get caught up in seeking approval from others. You're not for everyone, and that's perfectly fine. One exercise I have given to clients is to write a list of all the things you have accomplished, big or small, from as far back as you want to go. Sometimes, we forget the great things that we have achieved, and we need to remind ourselves of how far we've come.

8. **Building Your Tribe: Choose Your Circle Wisely**

    Create a supportive and positive tribe. Not everyone deserves a spot in your inner circle. Be selective and only include those who truly value and uplift you. This means establishing boundaries and deciding who gets to be a part of your inner circle. Remember, it's about quality, not quantity. Surround yourself with people who reflect the respect and love you have for yourself.

9. **The Power of Positivity: Take Control**

    Enough with the complaining! It only attracts more negativity. Shift your focus towards positive actions and thoughts. This mindset fosters self-love and fulfillment, propelling you towards your goals.

10. **Setting Boundaries: Guard Your Space and Mind**

    Establish clear boundaries. How you treat yourself sets the standard for how others will treat you. Don't let toxicity or negativity encroach on your space or peace of mind. Reclaim your power and focus on healing and growing.

11. **Self-Prioritization: Put Yourself First**

    It's not selfish; it's necessary. Prioritize your well-being above all else. This means taking the time for self-care, saying no when needed, and ensuring you're not running on empty. Remember, your value doesn't decrease based on someone's inability to see your worth. It also means paying yourself first (which we'll cover in Chapter 16).

12. **Raising Your Earning Potential: Financial Empowerment**

Finally, improving your relationship with money and increasing your financial confidence is crucial. It starts with taking control of your thoughts and actions and recognizing your worth in every aspect of your life, including your finances. Implement small, actionable steps to see big changes in how you manage and value your money.

13. **The Luxury of Confidence - Investing in Quality Underwear**

You're probably wondering, "What?" Indulging in good, sexy underwear, undergarments, or lingerie isn't about outer appearances; it's a deeply personal form of self-respect and empowerment. This might seem like a small detail, but it's a powerful act of self-care that boosts your confidence and makes you feel luxurious and powerful on the inside.

Wearing quality lingerie is a statement to yourself that you deserve the best. It's an intimate reminder of your worth and beauty, regardless of who gets to see it. This personal luxury subtly influences your posture, your mood, and how you carry yourself throughout the day. You move differently when you feel confident and valued from the inside out. You need to feel good. When you feel sexy, you feel good, and it reflects how much money you deserve, which in turn attracts better opportunities.

This past year, I have experienced the luxury of staying in beautiful five-star hotels, flying first class, and eating at incredible fine-dining establishments. I'm sharing this not to show off but to confess that it was occasionally difficult. I would feel this feeling of "Oh my gosh, this is so expensive. This is too much." And there was this tiny resistance. I felt a sense of guilt as it hindered my full enjoyment. Eventually, I had to work through that because I knew that part of that experience was rooted in the fact that my mom's money story and words are one of extreme frugality (a mindset I often catch myself buying into), and you know about me popping that Wonder Woman balloon that messed me up. Yet, I understood the importance of recognizing my own value and deservingness. I knew that if I continued to look at these moments of luxury and opportunity with that vibration, I was signaling, "Hey, it's all good. I don't really want this. You don't have to keep it coming." And that alone made me wake up and choose to embrace and enjoy the opulence with a heart of gratitude.

Remember, when it comes to building wealth, valuing yourself is the starting point for both material and relational success. Embrace your worth, work on your flaws, and don't be afraid to showcase the best version of yourself to the world. Your journey to financial and personal empowerment starts with recognizing and increasing your intrinsic value. And remember, indulging in personal luxuries like high-quality lingerie isn't just about aesthetics—it's a profound act of self-care that reaffirms your worth and boosts your confidence. Nice, quality things are your new normal. This subtle, personal decision has the power to profoundly affect your subconscious, serving as a daily reminder that you are worthy of financial success and a luxurious lifestyle. Embracing this form of self-care is a testament to understanding and asserting your value, attracting the energy of prosperity and success. Let this be a luxurious secret between you and your confidence, a daily affirmation of your worth that empowers you to demand and manifest the best in every aspect of your life. Let's get to it because, like L'Oréal Paris says, "you're worth it."

• • •

Chapter Takeaways:

- Embrace your worth: Living by your value transforms your self-view and financial relationships.

- Attract wealth with self-value: Valuing yourself aligns you with the abundance frequency, naturally drawing in wealth.

- Choose Your Circle Wisely: A supportive network reflects and reinforces your self-respect.

- Self-Care is Key: Prioritizing well-being and indulgences signals to the universe you're ready for success.

Action Step:

Set a boundary this week, whether it's saying no to an unwanted commitment or asking for what you need in a relationship or at work.

13 Follow and Love Your Creative Pursuit

"Design a future where your passions are pursuits and include what your heart truly wants to do."

JEN FONTANILLA

I'm sitting there, in the hospital, thinking: *No more joy or feeling the satisfaction of releasing my creativity. Nope, this is the logical Jen.*

In my TEDx talk *Artistic Dreams: Why you shouldn't give up on them,* I shared a pivotal moment from my life. I entered college with the intention of pursuing a career in the medical field. Yet, deep down, I felt an unmistakable tug in a different direction. This internal conflict isn't unique to me—you might know the feeling, too. That gnawing gut sensation, the whisper of the heart signaling a change of course. The doubts were daunting: Was I making the right decision? Would my parents be disappointed? Could I really make a living if I chose a different path?

The decision was frightening, yet what scared me more was the thought of ignoring my true calling. The prospect of living a life of conventional success while constantly knowing I had abandoned my real dreams was unbearable. That realization, both saddening and terrifying, spurred me to take the leap.

● ● ●

Through numerous conversations with others in creative fields, I've discovered a common thread: we all have grand dreams. We dream of creating, building, and producing extraordinary, joyful things that light and fill us up. Yet, often, we find ourselves swimming against the tide—battling societal expectations, parental pressures, and the skepticism of naysayers. It's an uphill battle marked by potential disappointment and, sometimes, shame.

But I urge you to shift your focus. Rather than dwelling on the expectations and judgments of others, concentrate on what you love and how you can do what you love. Consider what you genuinely feel you are meant to do in this world. When you make decisions from a place of love and true integrity—especially towards yourself—you align with your deepest purpose. Let this alignment guide you as you pursue your creative passions. Remember, when you operate from this core, your choices resonate with profound authenticity and give you the power and permission to do what you were placed on this Earth to do.

You are a remarkable creator, uniquely equipped with talents that the world eagerly needs. Every creative soul is here for a purpose, and yours is no exception. You have a distinctive role that no other artist, designer, writer, or creator can fulfill. This exceptional contribution is your life's masterpiece. When you engage deeply with your true calling, you align with your higher creative path. Embracing this journey will bring an enriching influx of joy, abundance, and well-being into your life, fueling your art and your soul.

As we immerse ourselves in what we love, wealth and prosperity effortlessly find their way to us. You might earn a living from work that doesn't inspire you, but it often requires more effort. When you don't enjoy how you spend your time and energy, it can restrict your flow of abundance. Conversely, when you love what you do, abundance tends to arrive more naturally and effortlessly.

You'll know you're engaged in your life's work when you feel a surge of vitality and aliveness. This profound sense of purpose will make your life feel more meaningful and confirm that your contributions are valuable. You'll be guided by a compelling vision or goal, and you'll notice an increase in happiness across all areas of your life. Your work will allow you to express your true self more fully and facilitate your personal growth and evolution.

When you tap into your unique skills and talents, you'll find opportunities to make money that not only fulfill you but also challenge and invigorate you. By doing what you love, you not only enrich your own life but also brighten the lives of those around you, spreading a little more light in the world. Embracing your life's work means you're achieving exactly what you were meant to do here on Earth.

Whatever your passion, it naturally benefits others—that's just how the universe works. When you harness your top talents, you're serving yourself and contributing to those around you. By fully dedicating your skills to your pursuits, your work becomes sought after, ensuring that money will find its way to you. Even if it doesn't seem immediately lucrative, trust your heart and stay your course. Following your true path will ultimately lead to greater wealth and abundance than any other route could offer. Trust the journey, trust in your higher self,and watch a new way living unfold!

Engaging in your life's work isn't just a career—it's a joyride to enlightenment and spiritual growth. When you love what you do, your tasks aren't just tasks; they become acts of mindfulness and joy. This blend of passion and attention not only enhances your daily life but also lights up your spiritual path.

Your higher self loves to chat, and guess what? It uses your feelings, imagination, desires, and dreams to do the talking! It shows you your life's work by nudging you towards what brings you joy and sketching out daydreams of what you love to do. Your life's work could be that thing you're always noodling on, feel deeply connected to, or are maybe even tinkering with right now. It might be the hobby you dive into during your downtime or that thing you always say you'd do if only you had more time or money. And the best part? Your life's work will make a meaningful difference, whether it's to humanity, animals, plants, or the Earth itself. It's not just a job; it's a way to give back and feel great doing it!

Your life's work often comes calling in the most delightful ways—through your dreams and daydreams about your ideal life. Think of these fantasies as little hints or playful nudges from the universe, pointing you toward what you're truly meant to do. So next time you catch yourself lost in a daydream, pay attention—it might just be your future calling!

Your soul doesn't get bogged down by who you are today; it's all about the big picture and all the amazing things you're capable of achieving in this lifetime. It sends you sneak peeks of your potential and the paths you could take through dreams about your ideal life. So, don't brush off those fantasies as just wishful thinking—they're actually VIP messages from the deepest part of you, showing you what you could do and where you might go. Honor these visions as the precious insights they truly are!

As this fresh wave of awareness catches on, you'll find yourself increasingly drawn to work that really fires you up and lifts others too. It'll challenge you to stretch and grow, offering you the exciting opportunity to bring a little more harmony and order to the world around you.

To sculpt your life's work, there's no need to feel pressured to do anything drastically different from what you're already doing. Pushing too hard usually just leads to resistance, not progress. You don't have to turn your life upside down overnight; you can build your dream career gradually, one step at a time. The things you're doing right now? They're planting the seeds for your life's work. What you're really aiming for is to flex those special skills more often and in ways that could sustain you now or down the road. As you lean into doing more of what you love, you'll find yourself cultivating the richest kind of abundance — a life that's fulfilling, vibrant, joyful, and overflowing with love.

As I sat there in the hospital hallway waiting for the next doctor to speak during my summer research project, philosophical Jen took over. It became crystal clear: abandoning my creative pursuits would mean leaving behind the profound joy and satisfaction that comes from expressing my true self. This realization was not just a personal epiphany but a universal truth that resonates with many of us in the creative fields. We are at our

· · ·

best — most alive and fulfilled — when we are engaged in work that not only challenges us but also allows us to contribute uniquely to the world.

Embracing this path is more than simply personal satisfaction; it's about bringing our whole selves to what we do, lighting up not just our lives but also those of others around us. It's about making a living, yes, but even more, it's about making a life.

As we turn the page to the next chapter, let's address the elephant in the room: fear. It's one thing to recognize your path and another to walk it amidst the fog of fear and uncertainty. How do we confront these fears? How do we hold onto our creative integrity in the face of financial worries or the daunting prospect of not living up to expectations? The next chapter will explore these challenges, providing strategies to harness your fears and transform them into stepping stones towards fulfilling your life's work. Let's continue this journey together, emboldened by the knowledge that what we're doing isn't just for today — it's for a lifetime of creativity and contribution.

Chapter Takeaways:

- Embrace your true calling: recognize that the greatest fulfillment comes from engaging in work that aligns with your passions and talents. When you pursue what genuinely excites and motivates you, it not only enhances your own life but also positively impacts those around you.

- Cultivate abundance through passion: understand that pursuing what you love naturally attracts abundance. Financial success and personal satisfaction are more readily achieved when your work is driven by passion rather than obligation or external pressures.

- Recognize the signs of your life's work: pay attention to the dreams, daydreams, and subtle nudges that point towards your life's work. These are not just whimsical fantasies but valuable insights from your higher self, guiding you toward your true potential and purpose.

Action Step:

Explore your daydreams: Regularly engage in intentional daydreaming about your ideal life and work. Take notes on what scenarios, roles, or activities consistently appear in your dreams. This creative visualization can reveal your true passions and guide your next steps towards achieving them.

14 Pursuing Creative Dreams with Fearlessness

"In the marketplace of ideas, selling is not conceding, but declaring that your creations have a place, a purpose, and a price."

JEN FONTANILLA

I wanted to write a chapter about fears because I think whenever it comes to selling something or having to present your work, which is a representation of ourselves, it always enters this scary territory. And then we have all these fears come up where we're concerned about judgment. We're worried about what other people will think. We have this fear of people not buying our stuff, and all these insecurities come up. And after being in both the financial and creative space for so many years, I know firsthand what that's like, and it can be very scary, but I have realized that it doesn't have to be.

And I think, as creatives, one of the things that we struggle with is pricing. Feeling that maybe we shouldn't be charging for something that is more of a passion project, or it feels like a hobby, or we have this idea that we shouldn't be charging for something that came out of our ideas, thoughts, and creativity. So, there are a lot of different things that we deal with that prevent us from stepping into our value and our worth - which, of course, affects the way we make money and the amount of money and wealth that we are so entitled to build and create for ourselves.

So, I really felt this section was important to address and not only talk about fear but some of the things that I have even done myself to help me work through this. As we progress and get better, we continue to elevate, grow, and provide more value, expertise, and experience, and that means you can ask for more in return when it comes to pricing. That becomes another level of fear where we don't feel we should be stretching ourselves and charging more. It presents an exciting new territory and an opportunity for more growth, as well as learning how to expand the container that enables us to welcome more wealth into our lives, which is a part of the whole process.

"But I hate selling!"

Ah, for many of us creatives, we have said it at some point, "I hate selling! Why do I have to sell? Why can't I just make things?" I mean, yes, you can, but you'll remain broke, and I'm assuming the reason why you're reading this book is that it's not what you want to become or a situation you want to stay in. So, here's the thing. I know selling can feel sleazy, slimy, and cringey. But here's the reality check: there's no way around it. You simply CAN'T run a profitable design or creative type of business without selling! So, let's try to look at selling in a different way for a moment.

Oh, I totally get it. How many times have we all been there, right? Groaning, "Ugh, I hate selling. Can't I just create stuff and not worry about the money part?" Honestly, yes, you could, but then there's the whole issue of being broke, which I'm guessing that's why you're here reading this. You want something different, something better. And hey, I hear you—selling can feel super awkward, kind of cringe even. But let's try to flip the script on selling for a moment, shall we?

If we're honest with ourselves, we hate selling because we're afraid. Own it. We're human and that's ok. It's almost like a running joke among us creatives that we're the worst salespeople, taking a weird kind of pride in that. Embracing the "starving artist" vibe feels almost noble like we're somehow more genuine if we're not chasing the dollar. It also feels like a safety net against that dreaded accusation of "selling out."

There's this widespread belief that creative endeavors are purely for the love of the craft. And, you know, sometimes that hits the mark. Occasionally. There's definitely a moment and a setting for things like jotting down thoughts in a journal, crafting a tale for a close-knit circle, or performing at a cozy poetry night.

But then, there are those moments when you find yourself asking, "I'm pouring my soul into my work. Why can't I see some financial love coming back my way? What's the deal?" There's absolutely room to shoot for the stars. If you've put your heart into something and it fills you with pride, sharing it with the wider world holds its own kind of worth.

Here's the kicker: a lot of the struggle comes from this heavy emotional baggage we lug around about selling. We've somehow convinced ourselves that selling = bad. I think we're also afraid because of a deep-seated fear of rejection. So sometimes we stay small. For example, we may only want to talk about our work with a small group of people because it's safe. Our mammalian brain and our subconscious mind is telling us to stay safe. We don't need to feel like we're being crushed by a larger audience.

Another way we may hide and stay small is to avoid marketing our work. Have you ever felt or said any of these words?

- "I don't want to feel like I'm imposing."

- "I should just lay out what I've created and then step back."

- "I don't want to be annoying."

- "I feel so insecure about selling my work."

- "This is my gift or passion. I shouldn't be making a profit off of it."

So, let's break it down, step by step:

- You create something awesome and decide to sell it.

- You let the world know, "Hey, this is up for grabs!"

- You internalize the fact that "Selling is helping."

- You let people exchange their money for your work.

Each step is just an action, and whether it turns out to be a good or bad vibe depends entirely on how we approach it. There's nothing inherently evil or saintly about any of these steps.

But because we're bombarded with sleazy sales tactics day in and day out, it's easy to start believing that's the only way to sell. It could also be a part of your money story! Did you ever hear your mom or dad say negative things about selling or a salesperson? "They're just trying to get our money and rip us off! All salesmen are crooks!" It's a part of that "All salespeople are out to get you" narrative that we've probably all heard at some point.

When selling goes wrong, it looks something like this:

- You churn out something shoddy or downright harmful.

- You convince folks they absolutely need it, regardless of the truth.

- You grab their cash with no remorse about whether you're scamming them.

Seeing this kind of thing so often, it's no wonder many of us start thinking, "Yup, that's just how selling works." Especially for us creatives, who tend to have our integrity radar dialed up to eleven.

But here's the thing: selling doesn't have to be like that. It can be totally in sync with your values, efficient, and, believe it or not, pretty enjoyable. Your work and your business can truly become aligned with your values and who you are.

When you're selling with integrity, it looks more like this:

- You create something genuinely valuable and beneficial.

- You find the folks who truly need it and clue them in on why it's awesome.

- You invite them to buy, trusting they're smart enough to decide for themselves.

This approach isn't rocket science, but it does require us to shake off those old, cynical views about selling and the folks who are good at it. Just because someone's nailing their sales doesn't mean they've sold their soul.

Believe it or not, selling can be as soul-nourishing as creating art itself. Embracing the selling process means stepping out of your comfort zone, confronting those gnarly self-worth demons, and believing in the value of what you're offering. This isn't just about getting comfortable with selling; it's about getting right with how you see yourself in the grand scheme of things.

If you've dedicated days or months to a project, then it's something the universe ought to experience. When you've invested your soul into creating something, it's likely nothing short of incredible. And if it's incredible, then it's something the world is in dire need of. We're all craving more awesome. By marketing what you've crafted, you're not just throwing something out there; you're contributing something magnificent to the cosmos. You're not intruding or pestering. You're presenting something magnificent.

It's true, but still, not everyone will appreciate it. Actually, the majority might not vibe with what you're putting out there, and that's perfectly fine. There's probably a specific group of people that your creation resonates with. In the business world, they call this finding your product-market fit. It's crucial to remember that if people don't connect with it, it doesn't reflect on you personally.

Tackling these challenges head-on transforms selling from a positive activity into something truly empowering.

Here's how that empowered selling mindset rolls out:
- You BELIEVE in the value you're bringing to the world.

- You STEP UP as the go-to person, showing others why what you do is unique and a solution to their problems.
- You lean into TRUST, believing in your heart that you're doing right by your customers or clients.

Selling isn't the dark side. Far from it. It's a golden chance to dive deep into your self-esteem issues, trust hang-ups, and overall life philosophy. Putting yourself and your work out there is gonna poke at all your sensitive spots, but if you're serious about making a go of it as a creative, this is the work that's gotta happen.

Let me tell you a story about Mia, a jewelry maker whose creations were more than just accessories—they were stories wrapped in metal and stone. Mia was terrified of putting her work out there, scared stiff of rejection and the nitty-gritty of pricing. Enter Lucas, an artist who'd walked the same tightrope and made it to the other side. He introduced Mia to a tribe of artists who believed in lifting each other up.

With a nudge from her new community, Mia took a leap and showcased her work at a local art fair. The response? Heartwarming. People were drawn not just to the jewelry but to the stories they told. This feedback was a game-changer for Mia. She began to see her work's true worth, and slowly, but surely, Mia transformed her relationship with her art and money. Sharing the tales behind each piece online, she connected with folks who valued her artistry as much as she did. Mia's journey from fear to fulfillment wasn't just about selling jewelry; it was about embracing her value in the world of art and commerce, all while staying true to her creative soul.

● ● ●

What I'm getting at is this: we've got to detach a bit from our creations and grasp that when we launch and market them, we're not pushing a "You must buy this" agenda. Instead, we're putting out a "This might just be your cup of tea" vibe and leaving it up to our audience to decide if it clicks with them. Pulling this off isn't a walk in the park. It asks for a breed of bravery that's not always easy to summon. But, if there's something you're passionate about—be it an idea, a product, a service, or an event—you naturally want it to find its people. And that effort to connect what you cherish with those who will cherish it, too? That's the essence of marketing.

Selling isn't just some tacky afterthought to creating. It's sacred. It's as much a part of the creative process as the creation itself.

What's next?

The topic of fears and limiting beliefs among creative professionals can uncover a variety of challenges that are unique to us. Creative individuals often face a set of common fears that stem from the personal and subjective nature of their work. Here are some examples:

- **Fear of not being good enough:** This is a common fear that many creative professionals face, often referred to as "imposter syndrome." It can lead to self-doubt and hinder their willingness to share or promote their work. I know this comes up often, especially when you're just starting out and getting your feet wet in the pool of creative work out there.

- **Fear of rejection or criticism:** Putting our creative work out there opens it up to judgment from others. This fear can prevent creatives from seeking feedback or opportunities to showcase their work.

• • •

- **Fear of financial instability:** Creative careers can sometimes be unpredictable in terms of income. This fear can lead to financial stress and may discourage some from pursuing their passion full-time. Fair enough, and there are logistical things that can be done to offset this. (We'll talk about that later.)

- **Fear of losing creativity:** There's often a worry about the 'well running dry,' meaning they won't be able to come up with new ideas or maintain their creative output.

To overcome this particular list of fears, there are different strategies creatives can do:

- **Practice self-compassion and mindfulness:** Recognizing that fear is a natural response and learning to be kind to oneself can help manage self-doubt and anxiety. Learn to be your own best friend and your most supportive person.

- **Build a supportive community:** I know that a few of the people I have worked with felt that the people in their lives, especially family and friends, didn't care about what they were trying to do. This made them resentful until they realized that it wasn't that they didn't care; it was more that they didn't understand.

  Connecting with other creatives who understand the unique challenges of the profession can provide emotional support and encouragement. There are even online and in-person communities you can become a part of, so you don't feel so alone or at least you'll get to hear from others how they are dealing with their fears and doubts. Oftentimes you just feel better being around other people who are "your people" and get you!

Your circle sometimes needs to change so that you can start attracting more like-minded people into it. I know, for me, some of my closest friends are the ones that I have shared struggles, wins, ideas, and failures with because we feel heard and understood together.

- **Set realistic goals:** Breaking down larger objectives into smaller, manageable tasks can make them seem less daunting and help maintain momentum. It's easy to fall into analysis paralysis and feel overwhelmed by a big project. I love to reverse engineer things by breaking up a big project into chunks and figuring out the tasks. I do this with my clients' big projects. I'll reassure them that our project isn't going to happen overnight, and I will give them the big picture of what we're building and the sections that we will be tackling. Next, I'll time block those sections and tasks needed to get those done into my schedule. As long as I feel I am making continuous progress, I will constantly feel like I'm moving the project along.

- **Know your market:** Understanding your market is crucial, not just for entrepreneurs but also for creatives building careers, even if you're not setting up a business in the traditional sense. How can you be truly confident in the value of your work, your pricing, and how you position yourself if you're not tuned into the dynamics of your market? Imagine any business owner leaping into an industry without a clear picture of the landscape—they wouldn't get very far, right? Similarly, as an artist or creative professional, you're not operating in a vacuum. Being aware of your market matters because your audience, whether they are clients, collectors, or fans, is paying attention. They're comparing, and they'll quickly sense if you're not clued in. This insight not only helps in tailoring your offerings but also in building a sustainable and recognized career in your field.

- **Level up your marketing skills:** After you've honed your message and deepened your understanding of your market, it's the ideal time to develop a compelling marketing strategy. Keeping a clear picture of your ideal client or audience in mind, start planning the content you can create and the measures you can take to overcome any doubts or questions your potential clients may have as they consider engaging with your services or content. This is your opportunity to increase visibility and interest in what you offer.

Begin this journey by identifying precisely what your ideal client or audience needs to know to make an informed decision about engaging with your services or content. Utilize marketing tools such as social media, your professional website, and email marketing to create and share content that addresses these issues in an engaging way, thus building momentum for your professional brand. Not sure what these potential concerns or questions could be? A straightforward and effective strategy is to simply ask!

- **Embrace feedback:** Learning to see feedback as a valuable tool for growth, rather than just criticism, can help improve resilience and adaptability. This one is huge! It's so easy to take things personally. Don't. One phrase I learned years ago was, "failure is feedback," and that goes for receiving criticism. When a client tells me they don't really like the way I did something, I just take it as "Great, at least we're moving forward," and then we figure out which change we need to make. This is a critical skill to learn because if we keep taking everything personally, we'll continue to stay stuck and miss out on potential opportunities and doing our best work.

- **Diversify income sources:** For financial fears, having multiple streams of income can provide a safety net and reduce anxiety about financial stability. I have always had income coming from different sources and different clients. One of the things I have taught my own clients is to find some type of steady work and continue to supplement it with other gigs and freelance jobs. If you can even find work that will put you on a monthly retainer, that's even better.

- **Believe you can make a living:** Your creativity is more than a passion; it's a potential career. Recognizing the value your work brings to others is crucial. It's about blending your artistic vision with a strategic approach to the market. Identify your audience, understand their preferences, and connect with them genuinely. This isn't merely about financial gain; it's about making meaningful connections through your art and earning a living in the process. By believing in your capacity to succeed professionally, you open up a world of possibilities. Embrace this mindset, and you'll find a fulfilling path that rewards both your wallet and your heart.

• • •

Extra Superpowers to Get Rid of Fear

Embracing Fear: A Guide to Moving Forward and Finding Peace

In "Power of Your Supermind," Vernon Howard hits on something pretty interesting about dealing with fear. He talks about the difference between the kind of fear that keeps you safe—like if a bear shows up at your door—and the kind that just holds you back from being your best self. His big point? It's about facing up to fears by seeing things as they really are, not as we imagine them to be.

Howard's pretty clear on one thing: trying to be totally fearless isn't the goal. Instead, it's about moving forward even when you're scared. That's the real way to beat fear. He introduces this idea of the 'supermind,' where you kinda step back and look at what's happening to you as if it were happening to someone else. This perspective can really help dial down the anxiety.

One thing he points out is how much our past fears can mess with the present. He's all about focusing on the now, cutting through the old, scary stuff that clouds our minds. And then there's this sneaky fear he talks about—the fear of nothing going on, which can get people all worked up when they're not busy. Howard says chasing distractions isn't the answer. Facing that quiet, that emptiness head-on, is where the real peace is. Basically, Howard is saying acknowledge your fear, roll with it, and find your calm in the now. It's a more laid-back way to think about tackling the things that scare us and living life more fully.

Stop Taking Things Personally

I'm not here to tell you to be emotionless or hide what you're feeling. Emotions are what make us human, and they're pretty awesome. Imagine someone throws a harsh word your way and it stings. I'm not saying turn into a robot and shrug it off completely. We've all got the power of choice, right? Picture this: you're chatting with someone, and they say something that cuts deep, and you feel it. You might even get a bit emotional.

What you gotta ask yourself next is, "How long do I wanna sit with this feeling?" It's kinda cool to let emotions flow through you like you're some energy field, and emotions just pass on through without sticking around. Because when they stick, that's when you've taken it to heart. Letting emotions flow helps you understand yourself better. It's like, what sets you off? What gets you stuck? It's all a chance to learn something about yourself.

When we let these moments mess up our whole day or get us all riled up, that's taking it personally. And here's the kicker: if something someone says or does something or some situation really gets to you and stays with you, it's like you're giving away your power to that person or thing. So, what's the trick to not taking things personally? Just ask yourself if you really want to give your energy to whoever or whatever is bringing you down. If you do, it's gonna drain you.

Keeping your energy and deciding to move past it is like hitting the power-up button on your life. It's when you shine, choosing your path and rocking it. So, give it a go, see what works. Maybe it's taking a deep breath, cutting ties with what's bothering you, or just reminding yourself of the awesome person you are and focusing on the good you're here to do.

Come Back to the Present Now

What does it mean to not feel fear? To me, it's all about rocking that confidence and letting your creativity fly. I'm talking about the kind of fear that freezes you up and stops you from chasing your dreams or just being your true self, it's usually because we're too busy worrying about the future.

We end up stressing out, feeling anxious or overwhelmed, and doubting ourselves big time. This means we're stepping out of our power zone in the present and clogging up our spiritual vibe. It's like we're telling the universe, God, or whatever you believe in, that we're not up for the challenge. This fear tricks you into thinking you're not good enough, you won't have enough, or you won't do enough. Or worse, you worry about people not liking you. It's a whole mix of thoughts that go against believing in yourself and syncing up with the universe. This fear? It's like you're denying your own unique energy.

So, here's what I want you to do today: notice if you're drifting off into the future. Is it a bright and awesome future filled with everything you want and that makes your heart happy? Or is it filled with worries and fears? If it's the latter, just remind yourself to come back to the present. Say it out loud, "I'm coming back to the present." But if you're picturing that awesome future and feeling thankful for it, then ride that wave! Feed into that positivity because what you think and believe is what you'll bring into your life.

Focus on Confidence

We often make life more complicated by piling on thoughts and emotions, which can trap us in a cycle of focusing on what we don't want, driven mostly by fear. This fear isn't about immediate dangers but more about the barriers we create that prevent us from moving forward and feeling fulfilled.

At the heart of our struggles is a deep-seated feeling of disconnection from the divine, leading us to seek joy and fulfillment in material things or experiences. While enjoying life's pleasures isn't wrong, relying on them for lasting happiness is futile because true happiness comes from within, not from external sources.

The key to a fulfilling life is to understand that our search for happiness shouldn't be tied to physical possessions or experiences but found within ourselves in acknowledging our connection to the divine. We are spiritual beings having a physical experience, and embracing this perspective can help us move away from fear and towards a life of joy and purpose.

To cultivate this inner happiness and fearlessness, focus on qualities like certainty, confidence, and joy. Use affirmations such as "I am joyful" or "I am empowered" to reinforce your inherent worth and connection to the divine. This shift in focus can lead to a more fulfilling and purpose-driven life.

Dropping Fear by Connecting to Higher Source/God/Spirit/Universe

Fearlessness is more than just not being scared; it's about really knowing who you are and what you're capable of. It's not the same as the instinctive fear you'd feel if you bumped into a bear in the woods. It's about understanding that deep down, you've got this spark of divinity, this 'God spark,' and when you tap into that, you start to see the world differently.

We're not talking about sitting around, hoping for the best without lifting a finger. Life's about taking action. But imagine how freeing it would be to let go of all that worry about what others think or the fear of taking a chance. Imagine just for a day, you dropped all those fears and just connected with your higher self, with that Source energy that's always there but gets clearer when you really focus on it.

The more you do this, the more you feel connected to everything—the universe, God, the energy around you—and you start living fearlessly. It's about realizing you're part of something bigger and letting that knowledge guide you to live your best, most fearless life.

It's essential for you, the creative professional, to grasp the transformative power of overcoming fear. Embracing your creativity fully means stepping beyond the shadows of doubt and into the light of your true potential. Remember, your art, your creativity, is not just a reflection of your soul but a valuable contribution to the world. Valuing your work rightly and charging accordingly isn't just about financial gain; it's a testament to the belief in your own worth and the impact of your creativity.

Let this be a turning point for you. With each step you take in conquering your fears, you pave the way for a more confident, courageous version of yourself. A version that not only recognizes the importance of selling and valuing your work appropriately but also stands proud in the knowledge that what you create has immense value. Your journey is about more than

● ● ●

just overcoming fear; it's about embodying the fearless spirit of a true creator, ready to make your mark on the world with your unique gifts. Let the world see your light.

Chapter Takeaways:

- Embrace selling as essential: shift from viewing selling as sleazy to recognizing it as a vital, beneficial part of your creative career.
- Value your work for pricing: recognize your creativity's value and adjust pricing as you grow, overcoming the fear of charging more.
- Diversify income sources: explore various revenue streams to reduce financial anxiety and build a more stable creative career.
- Focus on present moment: anchor your creativity in the present to control anxiety about the future, fostering a more focused and fearless creative process.

Action Step:

Identify the piece of your work you're most proud of but have hesitated to share or sell. Plan a small, personal showcase for it, even if it's just online or among friends, to start overcoming the fear of exposure and valuation.

BONUS MATERIAL

The **"CREATIVE SOUL ASCENSION MEDITATION"** is perfect for the creative who finds the business side of things like pricing and negotiating a bit tricky. It's super helpful for anyone who feels awkward or uncomfortable talking about money or questioning the value of their own work.

JUST SCAN THE QR CODE RIGHT HERE OR VISIT THE LINK BELOW TO ACCESS YOUR FREE BONUS!

SCAN ME

www.jenmoneycoach.com/the-creative-code-book-bonuses

15 | Setting the Tone for Each Day

*"Let each sunrise be your daily reboot, where intentions are set,
energy is chosen, and the universe aligns in your favor."*

JEN FONTANILLA

How you start your day sets the tone for everything that comes after. Think of it this way: everything around us, including us, is made up of energy. So, the kind of energy you start your day with? That's pretty much going to dictate how the rest of your day unfolds. If you're getting easily sidetracked, your energy is probably scattered. Feeling wiped out? Your energy's likely running on empty. But if you're feeling like everything's going your way, well, your energy's probably buzzing in the best way possible.

Now, why am I even bringing this up? I genuinely believe how you start your day, with a little bit of what I like to call an 'abundance mindset,' maybe a bit of reading, a walk, or some meditation, really sets the tone for your energy.

That energy you kick off with? It's going to weave through your whole day. Picture this: you could start your day diving into emails, scrolling through social media, catching up on the news—your energy's going to mirror all that noise. It means that your thoughts and feelings throughout the day are probably going to need a few moments, maybe even a few deep breaths, to reset if you start off on that foot.

Alternatively, by beginning with water, stretching, reflection, or a captivating book, you're creating a distinct energy for your day. This kind of start brings a richness to your day, making everything feel a bit more special.

The key is that we often overlook the fact that using those initial 15 to 30 minutes wisely is actually beneficial for our entire day. If you consistently dedicate time to uplifting activities, your days will feel more focused and smoother.

I love this quote from the late motivational speaker Jim Rohn, "Either you run the day, or the day runs you." If you start off reacting to emails and social media, it often feels like you're playing catch-up. But if you claim that time for something positive, you're also claiming more energy and focus for yourself. It's like making a deposit into your personal energy bank, ensuring that no matter what the day throws at you, you're more centered, more conscious, and just vibrating on a higher level.

For creative professionals, establishing a daily practice isn't just beneficial; it's transformative. It allows you to clear the clutter, tune into your creative frequency, and align with the universal flow of abundance and success. This isn't about rigid structures but creating a rhythm that sings to your soul, making room for abundance, and opening up to the wealth of your own creativity.

● ● ●

Connect with God, your Higher Power and Source, and yourself to set your day with the right energy. It's all about starting right to keep that easy, relaxed vibe going all day long.

How to Weave Magic into Each Day

Here is a list of different things that you can sprinkle throughout your day or even at the beginning of your day. My day consists of a mix of different activities until I finally go to bed. The misconception can be, "This is way too simple." And it is. However, are we doing it?

Starting with intention: Kick off your day by setting a clear intention. Think of it as setting the GPS for your day. What direction do you want to head in? How do you want to feel, and what do you wish to attract?

Incorporating practices from previous chapters: You've already explored a variety of tools—meditation to connect with your inner self, forgiveness to release the past, affirmations to reshape your narrative. Now, it's about making them a part of your everyday life.

Morning rituals: Begin with a moment of meditation. Let this be your time to connect with silence, with yourself. It sets the tone for a day filled with purpose and peace. Some of you may be thinking right at this moment, "I don't have time for this." Start with one minute if this is your first time trying this out, then work your way to 5 minutes. It's about what works for you. The important thing is to just start.

Affirmations: Follow up with affirmations. These are your power statements. Choose affirmations that resonate with your intention for the day. Say them out loud, say them proud. You've probably seen it often where people write them on Post-its and put them on their bathroom mirror or around their computer monitor. These serve as little reminders. Many creatives find that starting their day with affirmations helps set a positive tone and intention for their creative work. They can energize and inspire you right from the start.

Forgiveness and healing: Allocate some time, maybe during a midday break or in the evening, for forgiveness work. This can be journaling out your thoughts, a short meditation focusing on releasing what no longer serves you, perhaps a prayer to God, or any other method that helps you let go and heal.

Clearing your energy: Incorporating energy clearing techniques can be incredibly liberating. This might mean practicing gratitude, doing a quick meditation, visualizing your energy being cleansed, or using physical movements like yoga or a simple walk in nature to shake off stagnant energy. It can even be stretching and just moving after sitting all day at your desk, staring at a monitor. You can also practice cutting cords and deep breathing.

Boundaries and Self-love: Remember, creating boundaries is also a form of self-care. Ensure you're carving out time to do things that feed your soul, reaffirming your worth, and being mindful of who and what gets your time and energy.

Key Points to Remember When Creating Your Plan

One of the challenges that people I work with have is trying to incorporate these things into their schedule and not knowing where to start or how to plan it.

Be Flexible: Your daily plan shouldn't feel like a straitjacket. Allow room for spontaneity and creativity. This shouldn't feel super rigid, although let's be real—we are developing some discipline and habits here, but they are for our own good.

Personalize It: Tailor your daily rituals to what feels most internally aligning for you. Not a morning person? It's okay to schedule your meditation for the afternoon. Or perhaps you'd rather journal right before you sleep.

Consistency is Key: While flexibility is important, try to maintain a level of consistency. It's the regular practice that builds momentum and brings about real change.

Reflect and Adjust: Regularly check in with yourself. What's working? What isn't? Adjust your practices as needed.

By crafting a daily practice that resonates with your soul, you're not just aiming for a better relationship with money or an enhanced creative output. You're embarking on a journey towards self-love, forgiveness, and, ultimately, a life filled with abundance and creativity that knows no bounds. Let each day be a step towards that ultimate vision of yourself.

Putting it into action

1. Start Small

The idea isn't to overhaul your entire routine overnight. Begin with small, manageable segments. Can you spare 5 minutes after waking up for meditation? How about a 2-minute affirmation session while you brew your coffee? Starting small makes the practice less daunting and more doable.

2. Assign Time Blocks

Dedicate specific times of your day to these practices. It doesn't have to be long; even 10 to 15 minutes can be powerful. Perhaps it's meditation first thing in the morning, cord-cutting exercises during your lunch break, and a brief period for forgiveness work before bed. Blocking out time—even if it's just a little—ensures you have dedicated moments for these practices without the pressure to find "extra" time.

3. Integration Over Isolation

Integrate these practices into activities you're already doing. For example, practice affirmations while showering or doing household chores. Visualize cutting cords during your daily commute (if you're not driving) or while taking a walk. This approach helps weave these practices into the fabric of your day without them feeling like additional tasks.

4. Prioritize & Personalize

Not every practice needs to be done daily. Decide which ones feel most necessary for you right now and start there. Your needs might change, and so will the practices you prioritize. Trust your instincts and make adjustments as needed.

● ● ●

5. Use Technology to Your Advantage

Set reminders on your phone for your various practices. Use apps for meditation or affirmation guides. Technology can be a powerful ally in keeping you on track and helping you manage your time effectively. I have even made widgets on my phone's home screen for quick access to my favorite meditations for quick access.

6. Reflect and Adjust

At the end of each week, take a moment to reflect on what worked and what didn't. Did you find certain times of the day more conducive to your practices? Are there practices that you're consistently skipping? This reflection will help you tweak your schedule to better suit your lifestyle and preferences.

7. Be Kind to Yourself

Remember, the goal of these practices is to enhance your life, not to add stress. If you miss a day or two, don't beat yourself up. Each day is a new opportunity to engage with your practices.

What an example of your daily practice could look like:

- **Morning:** Upon waking, spend 5 minutes meditating in bed or somewhere comfortable. Follow up with 2 minutes of powerful affirmations while getting ready for the day.

- **Midday:** Use your lunch break or a midday pause for a 5-minute cord-cutting visualization. This can help release any stress accumulated in the morning and rejuvenate your energy for the rest of the day.

- **Evening:** Before bed, spend 5-10 minutes on forgiveness work, journaling, or a quiet meditation focusing on releasing what no longer serves you. This practice helps clear your mind and soul, promoting restful sleep.

Remember: The beauty of these practices lies in their flexibility. The intention is for them to be adjusted to match your life and schedule, not the other way around. With a bit of planning and a lot of compassion for yourself, you can weave these transformative practices into your daily life, leading to a richer, more creative, and abundant existence.

Oma, one of my clients, has made a commitment to journaling and meditation. I recall her leaving me messages about getting derailed but then finding her way back. With time, she realized the importance of going to bed earlier, setting time blocks, and dedicating hours to finding copywriting clients. She made it a habit to watch things unfold positively in the direction she had always dreamt of.

As we wrap up this chapter, remember that integrating these practices into your daily routine is a journey towards harmonizing your inner world with the abundance and creativity that surrounds us. By carving out moments for meditation, affirmations, forgiveness, cord-cutting, and setting intentions, you're not just crafting a schedule; you're sculpting a lifestyle that vibrates with creativity, abundance, and peace.

This isn't about mastering time management or adding more to your to-do list. It's about making space for practices that align you with your highest self and the universal energies that guide us. Each small step, each moment you dedicate to these practices, is a brick in the foundation of a life lived with purpose, creativity, and abundance. Let's embrace this journey with open hearts and minds, allowing the transformation to unfold in its own time and rhythm.

Chapter Takeaways:

- Connect daily with your divine Source: Starting your day by aligning with God or your Higher Power sets a profound tone of guidance, peace, and abundance for all activities that follow.
- Begin your day with purpose: Your morning routine determines the energy for the rest of your day.
- Make time for energy clearing: Practices like gratitude and physical movement help refresh your energy.
- Embrace flexibility: Your daily rituals should adapt to your life, not the other way around.

Action Step:

Choose one grounding practice—be it a 5-minute meditation, reading or writing an affirmation, or a visualization exercise. Then, take out your phone and set a daily reminder on your timer to commit to this act, ensuring you make space for this powerful moment of connection and intention every day.

16 Designing Your Plan for Creative Abundance and Financial Wealth

"In the journey from art to income, understanding your financial landscape is as vital as the passion that drives your creativity."

JEN FONTANILLA

As we venture into this transformative journey of melding creativity with financial prosperity, it's crucial to know what the next steps are and who can help you get there. This chapter is your guide, blending the spiritual and emotional with the practical, ensuring your passion aligns with prosperity.

Setting the Foundation to Build Wealth

1. Setting Goals

Imagine setting sail without a destination. That's what pursuing a creative career without goals feels like. Goals give you direction, motivation, and a benchmark for success. As a creative professional, start by dreaming big—what do you envision for your life and career? Then, break down those dreams into achievable goals, both short-term and long-term. Remember, goals are not set in stone; they're landmarks on your journey, meant to guide and motivate you.

2. Pay Yourself First

When you hear the phrase "pay yourself first," it might seem a bit out there, right? Like, of course, you want to get paid! But this concept digs a bit deeper than just splurging on the latest tech gadget or grabbing that extra-large coffee on a Monday morning. It's a foundational pillar of a healthy money mindset, emphasizing the importance of prioritizing your own financial well-being above all else. When you allocate a portion of your income to your savings or investments right off the bat, it's not just a smart financial move; it's a powerful statement to yourself and the universe that you value your future, your peace of mind, and your dreams. It's like saying, "Hey, universe, I'm betting on myself here. I'm important." This act of self-prioritization isn't selfish; it's essential. It's a reminder that before you can effectively care for others or meet external obligations, you need to secure your own financial oxygen mask first. By doing so, you reinforce the belief in your own worth and set a foundation that enables you to approach life and your financial goals with confidence and clarity.

3. Budget for Irregular Income

The ebb and flow of income can be one of the most challenging aspects of a creative career. Budgeting becomes your anchor in these fluctuating tides. Begin by understanding your essential expenses and setting aside a buffer for leaner months. This approach not only ensures your financial stability but also eases the anxiety that can come with uncertain income, allowing you to focus on your creative endeavors.

4. Get Educated on Financial Literacy

Financial literacy is empowering. It's about understanding how money works and making informed decisions. Invest time in learning about budgeting, investing, and managing debts. This knowledge is as crucial as your creative skills, enabling you to build a sustainable career. There are myriad resources available—from books, online courses, and programs—tailored to every level of expertise. Please do not make the excuse "I'm not good with money." That is just an excuse. Empower yourself that you can learn and will have control of your business, career and plans to make this happen.

5. Diversify Your Income Streams

Relying on a single income source is like walking a tightrope without a safety net. Explore various avenues to monetize your creativity. This could mean selling digital products, taking on teaching roles, teaching a workshop, or creating videos to teach others what you do. Discover methods to explore passive income opportunities. Diversification not only secures your financial foundation but also enriches your creative practice by opening up new avenues for expression and growth. Here's the other thing, too—you don't want to be stuck stressing out when one of your income streams stops. Trust me—it sucks, and it's scary. Depending on one thing to pay the bills is not secure, and it can possibly set you up for failure and stress (and we know that's just not a fun place to be in.)

6. Invest in Professional Development

Investing in yourself is the most profitable investment you can make. Whether it's attending workshops/seminars/conferences, enrolling in courses, or seeking mentorship, each step you take toward professional development amplifies your value in the marketplace. It's about honing your craft, expanding your skills, and keeping abreast of industry trends, especially anything related to tech, to ensure you remain relevant and competitive. With AI present, there are numerous ways to consistently enhance your current activities. I actually dedicate a huge portion of my income towards learning new techniques and finding out how to implement various business systems to make my life and business easier. Not only that, but it's also fun. It keeps my mind alert, I discover new things, and, oftentimes, it benefits my own clients. This leads to the next point below.

7. Build a Financial Support and Community Around You

No one thrives in isolation, especially in the creative and financial realms. Create a community of financial advisors, mentors, fellow creatives, and maybe an accountant. Each plays a distinct role in your journey—offering advice, sharing opportunities, and providing support during challenging times. This network becomes your sounding board, helping you navigate the complexities of a creative career with financial savvy. Toward the end of this chapter, I've included a list of different types of professionals and what questions you can ask when you consider working with some of them.

8. Practice Mindful Spending

Mindful spending is about aligning your financial choices with your values and goals. It's the art of discerning between wants and needs, ensuring that each purchase and investment supports your overarching aspirations, goals, and dreams. Doing this not only fosters financial health but also cultivates a sense of gratitude and contentment, which are the essential qualities for a fulfilling creative life.

9. Set Aside Money for Taxes

This is a significant mistake that I must highlight, particularly for contractors and freelancers. Taxes are an unavoidable part of professional life, yet they can catch you off-guard if you're not prepared. Setting aside a portion of your income for taxes ensures you're not scrambling when tax season arrives. Nothing is fun at the end of the year to discover that you owe the IRS a bunch of money and you don't have it. It's a discipline that reinforces your financial responsibility and peace of mind, allowing you to focus on what you love—creating. Make sure you are setting aside a portion of this aside if you are a contractor by consulting with a great accountant who can carefully guide you.

10. Financial Self-Care

Just as you nourish your body and mind, your finances require care and attention. This means regular check-ins with your budget, investments, and financial goals. Financial self-care is about maintaining a healthy relationship with money, one that respects your hard work and supports your creative ambitions.

11. Giving Back

Incorporating charity directly into your business strategy isn't just a noble endeavor; it's a transformative one. From the jump, consider committing a portion of your revenue—say, ten percent of your gross income (or start at one, something!) to go to charitable causes or your place of worship. This commitment reflects a deep conviction that by looking out for others, we ensure our own prosperity as well. (Think back to the universal laws and what we want to magnetize for ourselves.) For me, giving back has always been a cornerstone of my business ethos, serving as both a motivator and a means to make a tangible impact. This approach has not only blessed my life tenfold but has also allowed those blessings to multiply, enabling me to extend even greater support to the causes I care about.

This practice solidifies my relationship with money with a deeply spiritual dimension. I look at money not just as currency but as a tool for amplifying my inherent traits, such as generosity. By embracing this mindset, you'll find that having more money simply means having more opportunities to help others. It's a virtuous cycle that not only helps your finances to flourish but also guards against any self-sabotage in your journey towards attracting wealth.

We can view our financial success as a way to expand our influence and create a meaningful impact in the world, completely changing how we perceive money.

I understand that some of you may be thinking, "You want me to contribute?" I'm trying to just get by!" I hear you. I've been there. MANY times. Here's what I will say. Start somewhere, even if it's in the tiniest of ways. If we say things like, "One day, when I start doing better…" That one day might not ever come, and we're not taking into consideration the way the universal laws work. So, if it's not monetarily, what can you give with your time? Throughout almost eight years, I've been actively engaged with The Youth Center as a board member, whether through volunteering my time or utilizing my design skills, but I am always striving to give back. If not money, what other creative ways can you give back?

12. Paying Vendors and People You Hire Well and On Time

Valuing those you work with by paying them fairly says a lot about your character and business ethics. It creates loyalty, mutual respect, and a positive work environment. This approach not only elevates your reputation but also attracts like-minded individuals and opportunities, creating a circle of prosperity. When I treat other colleagues, vendors, contractors, and people I collaborate with respect - it shows that I value them and what they have to offer. This builds trust and rapport and often leads to other projects. But more importantly, it creates a wonderful synergy, which in turn makes things fun, especially because you most likely have a shared goal that you're working on together.

13. Have Fun

In Chapter 2, we touched upon this under The Law of Rhythm. At the heart of creativity is joy. Don't let the pursuit of financial success overshadow the passion that drove you to this path. Make time for projects that ignite your soul, experiment, and remember to laugh. Having fun also stems from building your network and community and that is how you can make sure that you don't feel alone or misunderstood during your creative journey.

Building Your Financial Dream Team

I gotta admit - the financial world can be pretty confusing, and I know firsthand because I had to navigate through the five acronyms and ways to describe the same strategy or product and translate the financial jargon. So, it's no surprise that so many of us get confused and don't know where to start. It's perfectly okay to admit and say, "Hey, I don't know how to do everything. I am so confused!" And listen, trust me, you don't want to do everything. Embracing support can be your secret superpower.

One thing that I learned early on when it came to taking care of my finances was to not be cheap and try to do certain things by myself. I consistently found competent professionals who provided guidance as I built my career and business. I didn't want to spend precious time in an area that I had no clue about. These things, like tax laws, retirement withdrawal rules, and filing dates, can change almost every year. Doing something wrong could end up costing you even more money than had you hired someone in the first place.

If I have a toothache or need professional teeth cleaning, I don't do my own dental work. I visit the dentist. The reason I emphasize assembling the perfect financial dream team is so that you can pursue creative fulfillment and prosperity without distractions.

I want to break down who can be part of your financial dream team and what each professional does so you can decide if it's someone you need right now or perhaps at a later point in your career or business. But I believe understanding this part can at least ease the confusion on who to talk to when you need certain help.

Important Note: You DO NOT need to hire and work with every single person on this list. As I said, it is confusing, and to add to that, just know that some financial professionals can often have two or more roles. For example, there are some CPAs who also have licenses to transact investments in addition to their tax planning business. Many financial advisors have licenses for investments but also can write insurance policies, etc.

Some even specialize in certain industries or a particular niche. Think of how some doctors specialize. Be sure to conduct proper research on each person's credentials and legal transaction capabilities. Financial professionals vary in their expertise, so it's crucial to ask the right questions about their services. (Included are questions you can use when approaching someone or following up on a referral.) Follow your gut instinct if you get that tug in your heart or stomach that says, "Eh, I'm not sure about this one. I kind of felt like they weren't really paying attention to what I was asking… it felt like they were giving me generic answers… it seemed like it was a cookie-cutter way of doing things…"

If you're saying or feeling anything along those lines, do not be afraid to interview another person or feel bad for not hiring them. This is your financial future. Oftentimes when we ignore these red flags, we go forward anyway and then go through very painful or unsatisfying experience and later we end up saying, "I knew it from the beginning. I should've gone with someone else." Trust that gut instinct.

It's important to explore potential hires, understand the distinctions between roles, and ask important questions.

1. Bookkeeper: *The Organizational Maestro*

Your bookkeeper is the one who keeps the beat, ensuring every penny in your financial symphony is perfectly placed. They're like your personal financial organizer, tracking your cash flow, categorizing transactions, and preparing those oh-so-important reports. They will track and categorize your expenses and collect all those receipts.

Questions to Ask:

- How can you help me decide if I need a bookkeeper or if I should tackle my books on my own?

- What's your bookkeeping process? Are we doing this together or do you do this on your own?

- Do you do this virtually or in person?

- What's your favorite bookkeeping software, and why?

- Can you guide me through understanding my monthly reports?

2. Bookkeeping Trainer: *The Personal Trainer for Your Wallet*

Not quite ready to hand over the reins but feeling overwhelmed by the DIY route? A bookkeeping trainer can be your guide, teaching you how to manage your own financial tracking with grace and ease.

Questions to ask:

- Which bookkeeping systems do you specialize in, and how can you help me choose the right one?

- What makes you an excellent teacher for someone diving into the financial details of my situation?

- Can you adapt your teaching to my unique learning style and financial situation?

- How do you charge for your expertise and guidance?

- What support do you offer if I hit a snag down the road?

3. Certified Public Accountant (CPA), Accountant or Tax Preparer: *The Tax Whisperer*

The world of tax legislation is a complex and ever-changing one. Tax professionals oversee your tax returns, ensuring accuracy and helping with tax planning, deductions, and compliance. But there are several different tax people in this category—the accountant, tax preparer, Certified Public

Accountant (CPA), and Enrolled Agent (EA). Each of these professionals plays a unique role in managing finances and taxes, but their qualifications, services, and areas of expertise vary significantly.

Accountant

An accountant manages and examines financial records, working across various sectors such as public accounting, corporations, government, and non-profits. Their tasks range from bookkeeping to financial reporting and analysis. While some accountants hold degrees and certifications, there's no specific licensure required globally to use the title of an accountant.

Tax Preparer

A tax preparer specializes in preparing and filing tax returns for individuals and businesses. Individuals with varying levels of expertise, including both basic tax course completion and more extensive certifications, can take on this role. The primary function of a tax preparer is to ensure accurate tax filings, and they must be well-versed in tax laws and regulations.

Certified Public Accountant (CPA)

A CPA is an accountant who has passed the rigorous Uniform CPA Examination and fulfilled the requisite education and experience requirements set by their state's board of accountancy. CPAs are licensed professionals who can perform audits, review financial statements, and offer tax planning and financial advisory services. They have the authority to represent clients before the IRS and They have to comply with a rigorous ethical standard, which encompasses completing continuing education to stay licensed.

Enrolled Agent (EA)

An Enrolled Agent is a tax advisor who is a federally authorized tax practitioner empowered by the U.S. Department of the Treasury. EAs specialize in taxation and have unlimited rights to represent taxpayers before the Internal Revenue Service (IRS) for audits, collections, and appeals. They earn their designation by passing a comprehensive IRS test covering individual and business tax returns or through experience as a former IRS employee. EAs focus exclusively on tax planning and tax resolution services.

Choosing the Right Tax Person:

- For general financial management and bookkeeping, an accountant might be your go-to professional.

- If you need assistance with your annual tax filings and your tax situation is straightforward, a tax preparer could be sufficient.

- For complex financial planning, audits, or if you need someone authorized to represent you before the IRS, a CPA offers the broadest range of services.

- When dealing with complex tax issues, needing representation before the IRS, or seeking specialized tax advice and planning, an Enrolled Agent could be the best choice due to their specialized expertise in taxation.

Questions to ask:

- How familiar are you with the financial nuances of my creative profession?

- Can you break down your fee structure? Any hidden costs I should know about?
- How do you approach deductions? Are we playing it safe, or are we adventure seekers?
- What's your strategy if my taxes land in a gray area?
- How hands-on are you with audits, and can you represent me if things get sticky?
- What qualifications and certifications do you hold?
- How do you stay current with changes in laws and regulations?
- Can you act as my representative before the IRS if needed?

4. Financial Coach/Money Coach: *The Life Coach for Your Finances*

These coaches are your personal finance cheerleader, either guiding you through budgeting, saving, and spending strategies that align with your creative ambitions. They're all about empowering you to make informed decisions that boost your financial well-being.

It's important to be aware that Financial Coach and Money Coach are terms that can be used interchangeably, but their roles and duties may vary. Some may focus on helping you create a budget or spending plan, and some (like me) may choose to focus on the emotions, subconscious patterns, and the inner work involving finances.

Questions to ask:
- Do you tailor your coaching to cater to personal, couple, or business finances?

- How do you incorporate the emotional and psychological aspects of money into your coaching?

- Are your strategies flexible, or is there a one-size-fits-all approach?

- How do you support me if I become overwhelmed or anxious about my finances?

- Tell me about your experience working with creatives and how you adapt your coaching methods.

5. Certified Financial Planner (CFP®)/Investment Advisor Representative/Financial Advisor: *The Architect of Your Investments and Financial Future*

Our financial future depends on what we do now, and this is where CERTIFIED FINANCIAL PLANNER™ Professionals, financial advisors, and Investment Advisor Representatives (IARs) come into play. Each plays a unique part in helping you manage your money, but they offer different services based on their qualifications and areas of expertise.

CERTIFIED FINANCIAL PLANNER™ Professionals are the all-around experts of the financial planning world. They've undergone rigorous training and passed extensive exams to ensure they can offer comprehensive advice. Whether you're looking to save for retirement, plan your estate, insure your future, or navigate taxes, a CFP® can guide you through all these areas. They're bound by a fiduciary duty, meaning they must always act in your best interest.

Financial Advisors cover a broad category of professionals who provide advice on managing your money. Some might specialize in investment advice, others in retirement planning, and some might offer a mix of services. The key with financial advisors is that their qualifications, services, and obligations to you can vary widely. Some may also adhere to a fiduciary duty, but not all are required to.

Investment Advisor Representatives (IARs) specialize in the nitty-gritty of investing. They are well-versed in the stock market, mutual funds, bonds, and portfolio management. If your primary goal is to grow your investments, an IAR, bound by a fiduciary duty to act in your best interests, could be your go-to professional. They work with or for registered investment advisory (RIA) firms and have passed specific exams that qualify them to offer investment advice.

To decide which professional is right for you, ask yourself:

- What are my financial goals? If you need comprehensive financial planning, consider a CFP®. For investment-specific advice, an IAR might be best. If you're not sure or have a specific need, a financial advisor could be a good start.
- What level of service do I need? Do you want someone to look at your entire financial picture or just focus on one area, like investments?
- What's my investment knowledge and interest?

Questions to ask:

- What qualifications and certifications do you hold? This question helps you understand their expertise.

- How are you compensated? Understanding whether they're paid through fees, commissions, or a combination can highlight potential conflicts of interest.

- What services do you provide? Ensure their offerings match your needs.

- Can you provide references? Hearing from current or past clients can give you insight into their working style and effectiveness.

- Are you more of a planner or an advisor, and what's your approach to investments?

- How comprehensive are your services? Do we cover everything from insurance to estate planning?

- What's your stance on Socially Responsible Investing (SRI)?

- What is your pricing structure for your services, and can you explain if there are any possible conflicts of interest?

- What is the frequency of our financial plan check-ins?

6. Insurance Professional: *The Risk Manager*

Insurance professionals tailor insurance solutions to protect you against financial losses due to unexpected events. Whether it's life insurance, health insurance, disability insurance, or insurance for your creative assets, they ensure you're covered so you can take creative risks with peace of mind.

Important Note: As a former Life Agent, I want to stress the importance of establishing life insurance as the first step in your financial plan, especially if you have dependents. It's important to have a proper life insurance policy in place to ensure financial stability upon your death. The mystery of our death's timing remains, but we should be prepared, nonetheless. It's the most loving thing you can do for your loved ones who are left behind. (I might be stepping on some toes to say this, but GoFundMe after the fact is not a financial plan. Please get the life insurance.)

Questions to ask:

- What is the method for calculating insurance coverage amounts (life, property, casualty, etc.)?
- What types of insurance are essential for someone in my creative field?
- How can I balance adequate coverage with affordable premiums?
- Can you provide guidance on insurance for creative projects or artworks?

7. Financial Therapist: *The Soul Whisperer for Your Finances*

A financial therapist operates at the crossroads of money and emotions, helping you untangle the complex web of feelings, beliefs, and behaviors that shape your financial reality. Whether it's exploring your money history, addressing financial anxieties, or rewriting your financial story, they provide a safe space to explore and heal your relationship with money.

Questions to ask:

- Can you share your background in both therapy and finance, and how you integrate these into your practice?
- How do you define financial therapy, and what balance do you strike between emotional and practical financial guidance?
- Have you done your own "money work"? What has been your journey with financial healing?

- What types of clients do you feel most aligned with, and what part of this work lights you up?

- What can I expect from our sessions together? Are we talking, analyzing my finances, or both?

Other Professionals to Consider Working With

Expanding your financial support team beyond the core professionals can provide you with a more holistic approach to managing your finances, especially as a creative professional. These additional experts can offer specialized advice and services that cater to specific aspects of your financial life, ensuring that all your bases are covered. Let's explore some of these key players:

8. Estate Planner: *The Guardian of Your Legacy*

An estate planner helps you map out what happens to your assets after you pass away, ensuring your creative legacy and financial wealth are distributed according to your wishes. They can assist with wills, trusts, powers of attorney, and health care directives, providing peace of mind that your creative and financial assets are protected.

Questions to ask:

- How can you ensure my creative works are preserved and managed according to my wishes?

- What strategies can you suggest for minimizing estate taxes and avoiding probate?

- How often should we review and update my estate plan?

9. Intellectual Property (IP) Attorney: *The Legal Protector*

An Intellectual Property (IP) Attorney is like the superhero guardian of a creative person's brainchild. Whether you're an artist sketching away, an inventor tinkering in the garage, a writer crafting worlds, or a musician composing the next big hit, this type of lawyer helps you keep your creations legally yours. They get into the nitty-gritty of copyrighting your songs, patenting your inventions, trademarking your unique brand, or keeping your secret recipes secret. Essentially, they do the heavy legal lifting so you can keep creating without worrying about someone swiping your work. Think of them as your behind-the-scenes partner in crime (well, in creativity), making sure you get the credit and the cash your work deserves. With an IP attorney in your corner, you're free to let your creativity flow, knowing your intellectual treasures are protected.

Questions to ask:

- How can you help protect my intellectual property and creative works?
- Can you assist with contract review and negotiations to ensure my interests are safeguarded?
- What should I do if my work is infringed upon or I'm facing a legal challenge in my professional practice?
- What experience do you have with cases similar to mine?
- Are you registered to practice before the United States Patent and Trademark Office (USPTO), if dealing with patents?
- How do you charge for your services (hourly rate, flat fee, etc.)?

10. Consumer Debt Advocate: *The Debt Defender*

Facing overwhelming debt can stifle your creative energy. Consumer debt advocates specialize in negotiating with creditors, managing debt repayment plans, and offering strategies to handle debt more effectively. They can help lift the burden of debt, allowing you to focus on your creativity.

Questions to ask:

- What strategies do you recommend for managing and reducing my debt?
- Can you assist in negotiating with creditors for better terms or lower interest rates?
- How can I protect my credit score while working through debt repayment?

11. Somatic Therapist or Wellness Coach: *The Emotional and Physical Balance Keeper*

While not financial professionals in the traditional sense, somatic therapists and wellness coaches can play a crucial role in your financial well-being by helping manage stress and maintain a healthy balance. Making sound financial decisions and pursuing creative endeavors are influenced by your emotional and physical well-being.

Questions to ask:

- How can managing stress and emotional well-being impact my financial decisions?
- What practices can help me maintain focus and creativity in my professional life?

- Can you provide strategies to integrate wellness into my daily routine for long-term financial and personal success?

Building a team of professionals tailored to your unique needs as a creative individual can empower you to navigate the complexities of finances with confidence. It's about creating a safety net that not only protects but also nurtures your creative and financial growth. Each of these professionals brings a different skill set to the table, addressing various aspects of your life and work. By thoughtfully selecting the right experts to support you, you're investing in your present and future, ensuring that you can focus on what you do best: creating.

The Simple 5 Part Money Plan

I know that was a lot, so I want to encourage you with something that I learned myself and have implemented. I love this because it's simple and doable and sometimes that's what we need to just start with because when it's complicated, we know we feel overwhelmed and never take action. And we're not doing that. So, here's the thing, I want to share a simple way to set yourself up so that your journey towards financial freedom isn't filled with anxiety, confusion, and missed opportunities. The key lies in a simple, actionable plan that aligns with both the universal laws of abundance and practical financial wisdom. This guide simplifies the essence of financial planning into five accessible parts, each dedicated to a specific purpose but together forming a holistic strategy for financial well-being.

Setting Up Your 5 Different Accounts

Here is how you can set up five different accounts as listed below.

1) **Personal Wealth Account:** Allocate funds here for your personal growth and future investments. It's about paying yourself first and allowing this account to grow, tapping into the law of attraction to multiply wealth. This can start off as a simple savings account and when you get to a certain amount, you can invest it. But this is money you do not spend. This is for your future. Paying yourself first shows that you value who you are and that you make yourself a priority. It's so easy to neglect ourselves so we start here and make ourselves and our future number one. When we do this, we show the universe "Hi! I take care of myself, and I can handle more abundance!"

2) **Fun Money Account:** Joy and pleasure should not be casualties of financial prudence. This account ensures you indulge in the experiences and items that bring you happiness, reinforcing the belief that abundance flows freely and enhances life's pleasures. It's not money that goes towards bills and debt - it's for fun and for you. I know for me personally, fun and adventure are important values that I incorporate into my life often. I realized years ago that it was more important for me to stop and pause and allow myself to enjoy myself because life cannot just be work and doing it for the future. There is beauty and value in enjoying the present moment each and every day. So, find small or big ways to bring that fun and joy into your life. Go take that spa day, sit in a fancy hotel cafe, and grab a cappuccino, or buy yourself that new tech

gadget that you've been eyeing. This is you splurging and welcoming more opulence into your life.

3) **Large Purchases Account:** Aimed at significant, often aspirational purchases, this account helps the need to resort to debt, embodying the principle of living within means while still aiming for the stars. This money that you're saving for that vacation that you've been dying to take, the car that you've needed because the current one is on its last leg.

4) **Charity Account:** Giving back is not just a noble act but a powerful affirmation of abundance. By allocating resources for charity, you acknowledge the wealth you have and your ability to share it, thus attracting more into your life. Earlier in this chapter, I explained what an important role giving has in our lives and how it blesses others.

5) **Debt/Investment Account:** This dual-purpose account serves to liberate you from debt while also paving the way for wealth multiplication through investments. It's about balancing the present with an eye on a prosperous future. This account can be approached in two different ways. Start investing only after you've paid off your debt. Or you can do both simultaneously. I personally prefer the latter because it could take a while until your debt is paid off and then you will have lost out on compounding interest depending on where you're investing your money. I believe it's better to get into the practice of investing, even if it's a little. It's in a sense also a way of paying yourself first.

How Much to Allocate

The distribution across these accounts is not one-size-fits-all. Based on your financial standing—from living paycheck to paycheck to enjoying disposable income—you decide the percentage of income to allocate to each account. The guiding principle is to start with what you can, even if it's as little as 1% of your income and put that amount into each of these different accounts or buckets, and to increase this amount as your financial situation improves.

So, if you're making $4,000 per month, 1% of that = $40

$40 would go into each of these accounts each month. $40 x 5 = $200 and that will leave ($4,000 - $200) $3,800 for your other expenses. Regardless of whether it's gross or net income, the important thing is that you're developing the habit of allocating money to these accounts for their intended purpose.

Conclusion

Embarking on this "Simple 5 Part Money Plan" is not just about financial management; it's a transformative journey towards abundance and fulfillment. By consciously allocating your resources to these five accounts, you adopt a lifestyle that cherishes growth, happiness, generosity, and independence. This technique goes beyond being a financial strategy; it is a manifestation of the lifestyle you aspire to—a life filled with experiences, contributions, and opportunities. Let this plan be the beginning of a future where your creative passions and financial prosperity align, leading you to the abundant life you deserve.

The Dream Budget

This is a fun exercise that I have done over time, and I incorporate this with a digital vision board that I created in Canva. I call this my Dream Budget. Many of the things that I would love to have, and they are usually some kind of tech system or program or app or even people that I want to eventually hire. It all requires money, a monthly subscription or one time investment. I write down my wishes and note the dollar amount needed or monthly budget required. Now I have a clear idea of how much money it would take one time or on a running basis to get this thing that I want. Now I can plan how many clients I would need, and how much I need to price out programs so I can calculate how many projects I need to sell and so on.

Next, I put an image of that thing on my digital vision board. I got to tell you - this works. On my digital vision board, I've included pictures of mentors and their program images. And many of these were five-figure programs that I have invested in. But I had the desire to do it and I planned. This is where the action comes in and goes way past gluing a picture of something you cut out of a magazine and sticking it to a poster board. There were so many times in the past when I wished I could've joined or invested, but at the time, it seemed impossible. My heart would sink, and I would be sad that I was once again set back from getting something that could help me move forward. The gratification of pinpointing my goals and finding a path to achieve them enables me to make a positive difference in more lives.

So, what is on your heart and mind that you want to enhance your life or work? Have you written down the specifics and the price? Sometimes making something happen starts off with just planning and just facing the numbers dead on. When we initiate that action, we start to think, "Hmm, perhaps this is actually possible."

In weaving together these threads—goal setting, financial literacy, diversification, self-investment, nurturing networks, mindful practices, and generosity—we create a tapestry rich with opportunity and fulfillment. By adopting this comprehensive approach, creative professionals can enhance both their financial success and their connection to their work and the world. Let this chapter serve as your compass, guiding you through the terrain of creativity and finance.

Remember, the most profound creations often come from a place of balance and intention. So, take these insights, tailor them to your unique journey, and step forward with confidence. The plan you create today lays the foundation for the abundance and joy that await you. Embrace this adventure with an open heart and an eager spirit, ready to transform our dreams into reality.

Chapter Takeaways:
- Knowing who does what is crucial for finding the right support for your specific needs, whether you're planning for retirement, managing investments, navigating taxes, or protecting your creative works.
- Before seeking professional help, take a step back and assess what you're really looking for. Your needs will dictate which specialist is best suited to help you achieve your goals.

- Set up five accounts for personal wealth, fun money, large purchases, charity, and debt/investment to implement a simple money plan.

Action Step:

Schedule a "Financial Health Day" within the next week. Dedicate this day to reviewing your current financial situation—your income, expenses, debts, and savings. Use this time to set clear, achievable goals for the next month, three months, and year, and identify who you need to work with to make these goals happen. This day marks the beginning of your journey to align your creative passion with financial prosperity.

BONUS MATERIAL

The "**BUILDING YOUR FINANCIAL DREAM TEAM GUIDE**" streamlines the process of assembling your financial support system. The same comprehensive list of financial professionals, their roles, and crucial questions for potential hires found in this chapter are now conveniently consolidated into an easily accessible document. This format allows for seamless note-taking and referencing as you build your financial dream team.

JUST SCAN THE
QR CODE RIGHT
HERE OR VISIT
THE LINK BELOW
TO ACCESS YOUR
FREE BONUS!

SCAN ME

www.jenmoneycoach.com/the-creative-code-book-bonuses

The Art of Prosperous Living
FINAL REFLECTIONS

As we wrap up this transformative journey, it's important to acknowledge the profound change that is beginning to develop within you. The path to financial enlightenment is both a discovery and a creation—discovering the spiritual and universal laws that underpin our existence and creating a new reality that aligns with our deepest values and aspirations.

This book has been a guide through the landscape of your inner world, where your relationship with money is not just a reflection of numbers in a bank account but a vibrant tapestry woven from your beliefs, emotions, and values. From understanding the art of abundance to raising your vibrational frequency, you've embarked on a quest to rediscover your creative essence and align it with the flow of universal prosperity.

You've learned to live by the universal laws, recognizing that your thoughts, feelings, and actions are powerful magnets that attract corresponding outcomes in your life. This wisdom is not just a tool for financial gain but a philosophy for a fulfilling life. Your relationship with money is now rooted in a deep understanding of these laws, transforming fear and scarcity into love and abundance.

The transformation of your money mindset is perhaps the most crucial step you've taken. By changing your money reality and beliefs, embracing forgiveness, and making space for creativity and abundance, you've laid the groundwork for a life of prosperity. The daily affirmations and practices introduced in this book are your compass, guiding you toward financial well-being and personal growth.

Your journey has also been about cultivating self-worth and recognizing the value you bring to the world. This newfound appreciation for yourself is the bedrock of your positive relationship with money. In this relationship, mutual respect leads to financial success, which is an expression of your true worth.

With your prosperity plan in hand, you're now equipped to navigate the practical aspects of financial management. Not only is this plan a guide to creating wealth, but it also transforms alongside your personal development. It's a testament to your commitment to live a life of creativity, abundance, and financial freedom.

As you step forward into your future, remember that the journey to prosperity is ongoing. There will be challenges and setbacks, but armed with the knowledge and insights from this book, you have the power to overcome them. Your journey is uniquely yours, a personal odyssey that unfolds in harmony with the universe.

To you, the creative professional, this message holds a special significance. You are the dreamers, the makers, the visionaries who bring beauty and innovation into the world. Be bold in your creations, fearless in knowing who you are, and unwavering in your belief that you are worthy of abundance. Always stay connected to God, Higher Power, Source,

Universe—whatever you believe to be the origin of all creation and the ultimate supporter of your journey.

Let this book be a beacon of light on your path, a source of inspiration and courage as you embark on your journey to prosperity. The road ahead is bright with the promise of abundance, creativity, and financial well-being. Believe in yourself, stay true to your values, and remain open to the infinite possibilities that life offers.

Prosperity is not just a destination but a way of being. Embrace it with an open heart and mind, and let the art of abundance illuminate every step of your journey.

Go forth with grace and confidence, for the universe conspires in favor of those who dare to dream and live with intention. Your journey to prosperity begins now. Congratulations on taking this significant step. Remember, you are a vessel of creativity and a conduit of divine abundance.

May your light shine brilliantly and your path be filled with joy, fulfillment, and prosperity.

Sending you love & inspiration,

ENJOYED "THE CREATIVE CODE"?

I'm on a mission to reach
500 REVIEWS and I would love your help!

If this book sparked your imagination or helped you unlock your creative potential in any way, then your review would mean the world to me! It's through sharing our experiences that we inspire others to embark on their own creative and wealth journeys.

Your review on Amazon helps readers like you discover books that can truly make a difference. And every review brings me closer to my goal and allows me to continue inspiring and helping passionate creatives like you.

Thank you for being a part of this community, debunking the "Starving Artist" stereotype and choosing a path of passion, happiness, wealth and joy. I am truly grateful for you!

SCAN THE QR CODE BELOW
TO WRITE YOUR REVIEW

Thank you!

THE CREATIVE CODE

ON amazon

JEN FONTANILLA is a Certified Money Coach (CMC)®, TEDx and international speaker, Certified Financial Education Instructor through the National Financial Educators Council and bestselling author of seven books. As a graphics genius, she has created designs for companies such as The Walt Disney Company, Sony Studios, Target and Nintendo. As a financial advisor she taught financial workshops for clients such as Goodwill and the U.S. Air Force ROTC and is a regular speaker at various organizations including University of Southern California and Children's Hospital Los Angeles.

With a unique skill set that brings together 25 years of experience in graphic design and marketing and 19 years in the financial industry, Jen helps entrepreneurs and professionals in the creative space bridge the gap between their mindset around money and their creative abilities. As they improve their relationship with money and themselves, they abandon the guilt and shame, reveal the confidence within them, charge what they're worth and create a life filled with prosperity, happiness, wealth and joy.

An ENFJ-A and 100% Aries through and through, Jen co-founded a hip-hop dance crew that's still going strong to this day. She is dedicated to her daily kickboxing before the sun rises, loves comedy clubs and magic shows, nursing a good Old Fashioned, and fantasizes of one day becoming a competitive Latin ballroom dancer or comedian.

Jen lives with her son in Los Angeles, CA, and together they enjoy hiking on different trails, flying to various countries and cracking up at Mr. Beast YouTube videos.

● ● ●